CROMWELL

ON

FOREIGN AFFAIRS.

CROMWELL
ON FOREIGN AFFAIRS

TOGETHER WITH

FOUR ESSAYS
ON INTERNATIONAL MATTERS

BY

F. W. PAYN.

LONDON:
C. J. CLAY AND SONS,
CAMBRIDGE UNIVERSITY PRESS WAREHOUSE,
AVE MARIA LANE.

1901

CAMBRIDGE
UNIVERSITY PRESS

University Printing House, Cambridge CB2 8BS, United Kingdom

Cambridge University Press is part of the University of Cambridge.

It furthers the University's mission by disseminating knowledge in the pursuit of education, learning and research at the highest international levels of excellence.

www.cambridge.org
Information on this title: www.cambridge.org/9781107594333

© Cambridge University Press 1901

First published 1901
First paperback edition 2015

A catalogue record for this publication is available from the British Library

ISBN 978-1-107-59433-3 Paperback

PREFACE.

THE *Times* newspaper of Feb. 18th, 1901, contained an article by its Cologne correspondent in which the writer observed, "The German hatred of England has never been greater than it is to-day."

Now in connection with this statement the author of these essays would make two observations. The first is that the one faculty which in his judgment is more essential than all others to anyone who wishes to apprehend the truth about international matters consists in being able to look at and to judge of facts in the *mass* as opposed to *details* and in preventing the judgment from being misled by those lesser details which are constantly being drawn like red herrings across the trail which is followed by the seeker after truth in international affairs. What are the most salient facts in the international politics of the world at the beginning of this century? The author would reply, "The rivalry for Empire between England, Germany and Russia." Now of these three nations we believe that the latter owing to the barbarism from which the vast majority alike of its peasantry and of its *noblesse* are but slowly emerging is not yet sufficiently matured to be in the running with the other two. Consequently we are brought to the question of the probable result of the contest for Empire between the English and the Germans and it is a question highly interesting for any Englishman worthy of the name. It is idle to deny the existence of that contest, alike in trade and in imperial concerns. It may be masked at one time or openly confessed at another, but it is going on all the time. It is but recently that the Kaiser in an unguarded moment of "ivresse" told the Reichstag when demanding more warships that "they were to be used against England, his great rival."

And again (vide the *Figaro*, Feb. 15th) in another such moment he spoke of "England the trade rival and the political adversary of Germany."

The *Times* of May 31st published a luminous letter from an Afrikander whose racial dislike of the English is self-evident, but whose eyes have been wonderfully cleared by the bitter uses of adversity. The words of people in this frame of mind are usually worthy of attention. He says: "If the English left South Africa to-morrow our land would be immediately occupied by the Germans, who boast that they can land 50,000 men per month in South Africa, all completely equipped, and that they can easily keep half a million of soldiers there for five years. I know now why that astute statesman the late Prince Bismarck said that Africa would be the grave of the British Empire. Between 1882 and 1888 he sent experts to the Transvaal to gather information of its mineral wealth. The German geologist and the foreign gold-mining engineer both agreed that the gold reefs of South Africa would prove far richer than any others ever known, and *German policy has ever since then been directed to getting possession of the Transvaal by any means and at any cost.*"

"Hence the constant encouragement we received to flout Great Britain. Hence the celebrated telegram to Kruger. The strong disgust at that telegram shown by the English was so unlike their usual humble submission to insults and interference that the hopes of the Germans to obtain the Transvaal without fighting for it were seriously upset. Then arose the great German craze to obtain sea power at any cost, for the Transvaal gold would pay for a hundred of the biggest fleets the world has ever seen. But fleets cannot be created in a very few years, however lavish the expenditure may be."

"The world had grown accustomed to see the British Government and people act more cowardly, currish, and submissive than the Chinese or any other people on earth, and no man living would have believed or could have foreseen that even a very small majority of English people would possess sufficient patriotism to endure war for any cause whatever if it would cost 20,000 lives and 60 million sterling. (Editor's Note. All this about "humble submission to insults" and "cowardly currish acts" merely spells one name—Gladstone. "If I had humiliated my countrymen before the world as often as Gladstone has," said Bismarck, "I should never dare to look them in the face again." To think of the mighty English people with Gladstone as their figurehead!) Therefore when the general election showed that a considerable majority of the burghers of England and Scotland were still loyal to their own land, even in spite of the war, it was necessary for Germany to temporize, so when Kruger arrived in Europe it suited German policy to flout him publicly. This was done to delay war with England *until the German fleets shall be strong enough to overmaster the fragments of the British Navy* which may remain after the big war which France and Russia will be cajoled into waging against England. Germany's one object is to take the place of England in South Africa. Germans love not the Afrikanders, but they love the African gold."

At a time when the English Press is but slowly recovering from a severe attack of Kaiser-mania (brought on by a cleverly-timed visit to this country), it is as well occasionally to look ugly facts in the face.

As regards the probable issue of the Anglo-German struggle the author believes that two passages in this book may be found to possess some significance, because the facts there set out throw light on the German national spirit. They are on pages 63 and 72. It is the difference in national spirit which alone determines the result in the long run.

INNER TEMPLE.
May, 1901.

CONTENTS.

CROMWELL ON FOREIGN AFFAIRS.

THIS essay has been written under the firm conviction that people who love their country and watch her destinies with real concern will find some surprisingly good reasons for considering the remarkable speech set out below. One of the peculiar charms of wide genius lies in the fact that its utterances are never out of date but remain as fresh and applicable at the present day as when they were first delivered. We think that the words of the Protector will show that this holds good in a very unique manner in this speech, which although it was uttered some 240 years ago may appear to some of us to contain infinitely more significant matter than can be found in the political speeches of the present day.

Let us consider for a moment the extraordinary position alike of the speaker and of his country at the time this speech was made and see how much Cromwell's position differed from that of some modern Cabinet Minister delivering a comfortable after-dinner speech on foreign affairs at a Guildhall Banquet.

" I look upon this," he said, " to be the great duty of my place ; as being set on a watch-tower to see what may be for the good of these nations and what may be for the prevention of evil." He had only reached that place by his military genius in a hundred hand-to-hand battles and skirmishes and he only kept himself in it in the teeth of a hundred conspiracies to get rid of him by death. Familiarity with attempts on his life by blowing up his bed-chamber, setting fire to his house, knifing him on the Hampton Court Road, etc. had bred in him such contempt that elsewhere he casually refers to them as " such-like little fiddling things."

Is it not natural that the speech of a man who had been through so much should be of rather an unusual kind and more noteworthy for subject-matter than for style? "I profess unto you," he says, "that I have made this speech not as a rhetorician " and " I have no rule of speech."

Imagine a man who had battered down 50 royalist castles and had fought many battles in which failure meant certain death haranguing the Commons for four hours and fifteen minutes on the Constitution of Ireland as a certain statesman has done in our own day. The thing would have been impossible. In comprehending this speech the first thing to be noted is that the speaker was not in any way primarily "an old Parliamentary hand" but he was what we English admire perhaps more than any other nation, he was a tried, successful general and man of action, with an amazing insight into national and foreign affairs and, as his rough genuine speeches show us, with an unselfish and generous heart, which forms a combination so rarely seen that when found it is worth noting. As regards the effect on national prosperity of the rule of the two different kinds of statesmen represented by the Protector and by the "old Parliamentary hand" aforesaid—it may be noted in passing that the one indisputably made us a first-class power in Europe and founded our modern Empire, whereas the other by his African policy (however good his motives) was the means of bringing that Empire to the verge of dissolution.

As to the position of his country among the nations at the time of the Protector's speech, it had very much in common with that position at the present day. There was as little room for doubting the danger to the country from abroad as there was to doubt the danger to the Protector at home. We were not loved any better on the continent then than we are now.

"Do look on the other side of the water," says the Protector, "you have neighbours there, some that have professed malice enough against you. I think you are fully satisfied in that."

Speaking of a foreign invasion of England, he says, " Think upon it, this is in design. If you will go and ask the poor mariner in his red cap and coat you will hardly find in any ship but they will tell you this is designed against you. So obvious is it by this and other things that you are the object (of their hate).......Should a (general) peace be made on the continent then will England be the general object of all the fury and wrath of all the enemies of God and our religion in the world.......If all the Protestants in Europe had had but one head that head had been cut off and so an end of the whole."

The Protector divides his speech into two parts. He first considers foreign affairs and then he turns to home affairs. His treatment of foreign affairs is so luminous and prophetic and it casts such a light at the same time on the novel principles of statecraft on which he acted that we are fain to agree with Carlyle that it would be hard to find anything like it outside the Bible. Here, if anywhere, the homely words and unpolished sentences express the feelings of anger, pity and kindness undiluted and warm from the heart. " Cut these words and they will bleed." The speech is rather that of an enlightened seer than that of a politician and yet the speaker never seems to leave the firm ground or lose his grasp of the solid facts of the situation, as may be seen by his remarks on our shipping trade, on our army, and on an invasion. His words, in Emerson's phrase, glitter with pictorial power.

We shall now briefly notice the chief utterances of the Protector on which we have based the foregoing remarks, and after a brief allusion to Carlyle's view of the Protector as contrasted with that of John Morley shall set out the speech, as revised and commented on by the former, to speak for itself, as it is well able to do.

I. The Protector's opinion of Dutch character and Dutch national prospects.

This topic is placed first on the list as the British nation has recently had occasion to occupy its mind a good deal about the same thing.

Let us hear what the Protector and Carlyle also thought of the Dutch.

" Charles X. of Sweden hath adventured his all against the Popish interest in Poland......He is now reduced into a corner : and what addeth to the grief of all, more grievous than all that hath been spoken of before (I wish it may not be too truly said) is that men of our religion forget this, and seek his ruin (Dutch and Danes)......Men that are not true to the religion we profess......God will find them out ! (Carlyle—The low-minded Dutch pettifogging for ' Sound Dues,' for ' Possession of the Sound ' and mere shopkeeper lucre !)......If they can shut us out of the Baltic Sea and make themselves masters of that where is your trade ? Where will you be able to challenge any right by sea ?... . I had rather you would trust your enemy than some friends, that is, rather believe your enemy and trust him that he means your ruin than have confidence in some who perhaps may be in some alliance with you (Carlyle—We have watched the Dutch and their dealings in the Baltic lately), I could perhaps enforce this with some particulars......The business then was : The Dutch needed Queen Elizabeth of famous memory for their protection. They had it, had protection from her. I hope they will never ill requite it! For if they should forget either the kindness that was then shown them (which was their real safety) or the desires this nation hath had to be at peace with them—truly I believe whoever exercises any ingratitude in this sort will hardly prosper in it (Carlyle—He cannot, your Highness, unless God and His Truth be a mere hearsay of the market, he never can).

"But this may awaken you. It is certain they (these Dutch) have professed a principle which, thanks be to God, we never knew. They will sell arms to their enemies and lend their ships to their enemies. They will do so. Let everything weigh with your spirits as it ought, and we must tell you, we do know that this of their having such a principle is true. I dare assure you of it, and I think if but your exchange here in London were resorted to, it would let you know, as clearly as you can desire to know, that they have hired sloops, I think they call them, or some other name. They let sloops on hire, to transport upon you four thousand foot and a thousand horse upon the pretended interest of that young man that was the late King's son."

So much for the Protector's opinion of the principles of the Dutch as a nation. Two hundred and forty years have passed since then and the world has witnessed the truth of the Protector's words and the gradual fulfilment of the Protector's prediction. The "low-minded Dutch" with their eagerness for lucre before everything else have slowly gone down the hill while the English have gone up it and have proved again and again that they were the better race.

Cromwell had no idea of separating his religion from his practical politics. "We have known well," he says, "the Protestant cause is accounted the honest and religious interest of this Nation." And then he goes on to mention the money the nation had parted with and the "just sense" it had had of the sufferings of the Waldenses. His cosmopolitan sympathy with foreign Protestants was unbounded. He believed that their interests were not only his but those of the English nation also. He says, " But it may be said ' This is a great way off'—in the extremest parts of the world. What is that to us? If it be nothing to you, let it be nothing to you—I have told you it *is* somewhat to you—It concerns all your religions and all the good interests of England."

2. AUSTRIA AND POLAND.

" Look how the House of Austria on both sides of Christendom, both in Austria and Spain, is armed and prepared to destroy the whole Protestant interest. Is not (the future Emperor) the son of a father whose principles, interest, and personal conscience guided him to exile all the Protestants out of his own country? And news daily reaches us that the Protestants are tossed out of Poland into the Empire and out thence whither they can fly to get their bread, and are ready to perish for want of food."

The later history of these two countries does not form a very cheerful picture, whether we look at Poland, thrice partitioned among its neighbours and then annihilated altogether, or at Austria, harassed by Magyar revolutions, decadent, priest-ridden and often on the verge of bankruptcy. The Protector's opinion of them does not seem to have been far wrong.

3. ITALY AND SPAIN.

" And what think you of the other side of Europe, Italy, Spain, Piedmont, etc.? They all—What are they but a prey of the Spanish power and interest? And look to that that calls itself the Head of all this! A Pope fitted to accomplish this bloody work. He influences all the Powers to this very thing " (destruction of Protestants).

The history of Italy and Spain from that time to this is also not a very inspiriting affair. As late as the middle of this century it was possible for a French statesman to say that Italy was "merely a geographical expression" and in our own time we have witnessed the more or less rapid decay of the remains of the Spanish Empire. The history of Austrian and French interventions in Italy does not form a bright picture of national life. At the beginning of the century Napoleon, who usually knew his men, said "There are eighteen millions of people in Italy, yet it is with difficulty that I have found two men among them."

During a large part even of the 19th century the Peninsula has been given over to brigandage and chaos.

4. ENGLAND.

The Protector's idea of the ultimate basis of England's power is also noteworthy. He thinks it lies in our national sincerity.

"Men that are not true," he says, "to the religion we profess, profess—I am persuaded—with greater truth, uprightness and sincerity than it is professed by any collected body, so nearly gathered together as these nations are in all the world"—and later he says—"In my conscience I know not for what else you are so hated by the Powers of Europe, but because of the purity of the profession amongst you, who have not yet made it your trade to prefer your profit before your godliness but reckon godliness the greater gain." Our history from that day to this as contrasted with that of the powers he mentions is no bad commentary on the Protector's opinion.

5. SWEDEN.

"Who is there that holdeth up his head to oppose this danger? (from persecuting Popish princes). A poor prince (Charles X., King of Sweden, attacked by Denmark and Holland), indeed poor, but a man in his person as gallant and truly I think I may say as good as any these last ages have brought forth ; a man that hath adventured his all against the Popish interest in Poland and made his acquisition still good there for the Protestant religion."

The few English readers of Voltaire's brilliant work on Charles XII. will find that the grandson of the King here mentioned made a considerable flutter in the Papal dovecots of Poland, Saxony, Austria, etc.   None of those countries could withstand him.   He overcame Denmark, Poland and Saxony, and struck such terror into the Austrian breast that the Emperor confessed he was under the King's orders.

6.   FRANCE.

There is no doubt that the Protector was well disposed to the French and thought better of them than of the rest of the continental nations.   In another speech he says they were the only Catholic nation with whom he could enter into a binding treaty because they would not, like the rest, break it at the bidding of the Pope.

Here also he says—" Really, were it not that France (give me leave to say it) is a balance against that interest, England would be the general object of the fury of all the enemies of our religion in the world."

The French remained in amity with the Protector while he lived and, after all, they have had far finer chapters in their history than the nations whom Cromwell condemned.   After the Protector's life was ended and there was nothing more to be feared from the " dead lion," there is a recorded act of Cardinal Mazarin which shows that when all is said about diplomatic insincerity and interested motives, diplomatists like everyone else can feel reverence and regard for the heroic dead.   At the Peace of the Pyrenees the Cardinal sent his carriages a day's journey to meet the Commonwealth ambassador but flatly refused to meet the future Charles II. at all, although he probably knew as well as anyone that he was likely to reach the English throne.

7. IRELAND AND SCOTLAND.

The Protector showed a very correct insight into the future of the two nations. In Ireland his chief hope lay in the company of Scotch who had settled in the north (now known as Orangemen) who, as everybody knows, now enjoy most of the financial prosperity that can be found in Ireland.

Those who desire a clue to the woes of that distressful country which annually occupies about half the time of the English Parliament with its affairs may find some light in the concluding words of the Protector, when he says that if the English run away "the Irish must possess the country again for a receptacle to the Spanish interest."

It was this same Spanish interest which was striving for the destruction of Oliver and of the English Puritan prosperity and with this same interest the Irish were and have continued hand-in-glove ever since.

How could the English be expected to treat such a people, since they had become what they were in despite of all the force and efforts of that interest to the contrary? The Smithfield fires when Philip of Spain was Prince Consort and the Spanish Armada had cured the English of philosophic doubts about the nature of that interest.

"You have a company of Scots in the North of Ireland (forty or fifty thousand of them settled there) who I hope are honest men. In the Province of Galway almost all the (rebel) Irish transplanted to the West (now in 1900 known as 'the congested districts' and in a notable condition with boycotting and Land Leagues) you have the interest of England newly begun to be planted—and should the soldiers run upon free-quarter there—upon your English planters as they must—the English planters must go through mere beggary and that which hath been the success of so much blood and treasure to get that country into your hands, what can become of it, but that the English must needs run away for pure beggary, and that the Irish must possess the country again for a receptacle to the Spanish interest?"

In Scotland the Protector's great hope lay in the rise of the middle class which as everyone knows is now among the most thrifty and intelligent in the world.

"In good earnest I do think the Scots nation have been under as great a suffering......as any people as I have named to you. I do think truly they are a very ruined nation and yet in a way hopeful enough. The meaner sort in Scotland live as well and are likely to come into as thriving a condition under your Government as when they were under their own great Lords who treated them no better than the peasants of France. The middle sort of people do grow up there into such a substance as makes their lives comfortable if not better than they were before."

Such were Cromwell's ideas about the nations by which he was surrounded and we leave it to the reader to judge whether or no there be anything in them prophetic or illuminated.

Within the last year there has been a debate in the Commons on the Protector and Mr John Morley has produced a book on him.

The debate was chiefly noticeable for the mild and patronizing speech of Mr Balfour, the Leader of the House, who suggested that the Protector's modern reputation was merely the creation of Carlyle's brain, and that Cromwell stood out in history as "a pathetic and *somewhat ineffectual* figure." In view of Mr Balfour's share in the management of the late war and of his Manchester speeches thereon we forbear from comment on this singular utterance. *Res ipsa loquitur.* Mr Morley's volume, although in places it is lucid enough, is in the main the comment of a paper-constitution-builder and gen-de-lettres (purely and simply) on the difficult and harassing career of a great general and statesman in times of civil chaos and rebellion. The world is loaded with such books already and we feel tempted to exclaim, in the words of Themistocles to the Eretrian, "What! hast thou too something to say about war?"[1] Mr Morley shudders at what he calls "the daimonic voice" of the soldier-statesman in dissolving his last Parliament without ceremony. Yet how can we wonder at his impatience when we remember that most of the members of this same Parliament spent a whole winter session debating daily about the fate of a poor lunatic named Naylor who thought that he was Jesus Christ, and then sentenced him, against Cromwell's wish, to mutilation of a revolting and barbarous description?

If we were asked to contrast Carlyle's with Morley's *Cromwell*, we should say that a single one of Carlyle's earth-shaking comments on the "speeches" has in it more that is perennial than Morley's whole volume.

The speech set out below has been abbreviated somewhat although the sense is never altered thereby. It will have an added interest when we remember that it was spoken by a man who was already beginning to be enwrapped by the great shadow of death. It was almost the last speech he uttered before he was removed from sight and while reading it we feel that he himself knew he was about to end his task and leave the English people that he loved so well. "Never," says Carlyle, "while this man lived did English Puritanism bow its head to any created thing."

---

[1] The above remarks are not less in point after the sentimental vapourings of Mr Morley in the *Times* on the supposed burning of Boer farms by the British soldiery. Mr Morley probably drew his inspiration on this subject from that nauseous well of unpatriotic cant, the *Review of Reviews*. For our part we contend that the wounds and death which have befallen so many of the gallant rank-and-file through the folly of their leaders in treating a crew of treacherous and fanatical enemies as if they were all members of the Ranelagh Club in point of honour is as much a crime on the part of the persons responsible as excess of brutality would have been. The only difference lies in the fact that the sufferers have unfortunately been our own men. Cromwell knew nothing of such folly as "rose-water wars."

Speech 17.

My Lords and Gentlemen of the two Houses of Parliament..........The impression of the weight of those affairs and interests for which we are met together is such that I could not with a good conscience satisfy myself if I did not remonstrate to you somewhat of my apprehensions of the state of affairs of these nations; together with the proposal of such remedy as may occur, to the dangers now imminent upon us.

I conceive the well-being, yea, the being of these nations is now at stake. If God bless this meeting—our tranquillity and peace may be lengthened out to us; if otherwise I shall offer it to your consideration, by the time I have done, whether there be, humanly speaking, so much as a possibility of discharging that trust which is incumbent upon us for the safety and preservation of these nations.

When I have told you my thoughts I shall leave it to such an operation on your hearts as it shall please God Almighty to work upon you.

I look upon this to be the great duty of my place; as being set on a watch-tower to see what may be for the good of these nations and what may be for the preventing of evil.

We shall hardly set our shoulders to this work, unless it shall please God to work some conviction upon our hearts that there is need of our most serious and best counsels at such a time as this is.

I have not prepared any "rule of speech" but shall only speak plainly and honestly to you out of such conceptions as it hath pleased God to set upon me.

We have not been now four years and upwards in this Government, to be totally ignorant of what things may be of the greatest concernment to us. Your dangers, for that is the head of my speech, are either with respect to affairs abroad and their difficulties, or to affairs at home and their difficulties. You are come now, as I may say, into the end of as great difficulties and straits as, I think, ever nation was engaged in. I had in my thoughts to have made this the method of my speech. To have let you see the things which hazard your being and those which hazard your well-being. But when I came seriously to consider better of it, I thought as your affairs stand, all things would resolve themselves into very being. You are not a nation, you will not be a nation, if God strengthen you not to meet these evils that are upon us.

First, from abroad......I do believe, he that looks well about him and considereth the estate of the Protestant affairs all Christendom over, he must needs say and acknowledge that the grand design now on foot, in comparison with which all other designs are but low things, is, whether the Christian world shall be all Popery, or whether God hath a love to, and we ought to have a love to and a brotherly fellow-feeling of, the interests of all the Protestant Christians in the world. (Carlyle—Yes, your Highness, the raging sea shut out by your labour and valour and death-peril—with what indifference do we now, safe at two centuries' distance, look back upon it, hardly audible so far off—ungrateful as we are.) He that strikes at but one species of a general (at one limb of a body) strikes at all. Is it not so now that the Protestant cause and interest abroad is struck at, and is, in opinion and apprehension, quite under foot, trodden down? Judge with me a little, I beseech you, whether it be so or no, and then I will pray you consider how far we are concerned in that danger, as to our very being.

We have known very well, the Protestant cause is accounted the honest and religious interest of this nation. It was not trodden under foot all at once, but by degrees—that this interest might be consumed as with a canker insensibly, as Jonah's gourd was, till it was quite withered. *It is at another rate now.* (Has this passage no meaning for our modern ears? Let us go to the High Church five minutes

from our door and hear what our children are being taught.)
For certainly this, in the general, is the fact. The Papacy and
those that are upholders of it, they have openly and avowedly
trodden God's people under foot on this very motion and
account that they were Protestants. The money you parted
with in that noble charity which was exercised in this nation,
and the just sense you had of those poor Piedmonts, was
satisfaction enough to yourselves of this, that if all the
Protestants in Europe had had but one head, that head
had been cut off and so an end of the whole.

But is this of Piedmont all? No, look how the House
of Austria, on both sides of Christendom, both in Austria
and Spain are armed and prepared to destroy the whole
Protestant interest. Is not (the future Emperor) the son of
a father whose principles, interest and personal conscience
guided him to exile all the Protestants out of his own
Country? (Ferdinand II., his grandfather......not a good
kindred that!) And news daily reaches us that the Protestants are tossed out of Poland into the Empire and out
thence whither they can fly to get their bread, and all ready
to perish for want of food. (There was no doubt about the
danger of being a Protestant then, "tossed out of Poland and
ready to perish for want of food.") And what think you of
the other side of Europe, Italy, Spain, Piedmont, etc.? They
all—what are they but a prey of the Spanish power and
interest? And look to that that calls itself (neuter gender)
the Head of all this, a Pope fitted—I hope indeed born not
"in" but "out of" "due time"—to accomplish this bloody work;
so that he may fill up his cup to the brim and make himself
ripe for judgment (somewhat grim of look, your Highness).
He doth as he hath always done. He influences all the
powers, all the princes of Europe to this very thing (Carlyle,
Rooting out of the Protestants—The sea which is now scarcely
audible to us, two safe centuries off, how it roars and devour-
ingly rages while this valiant one is heroically bent to bank it
in. He prospers, he does it, flings his life into the gap—that

we for all coming centuries may be safe and ungrateful), and no man like this present man (Alexander I. "an able Pope," Dryasdust informs me). So that I beseech you, what is there in all the parts of Europe but a consent, a cooperating at this very time and season "of all Popish powers" to suppress everything that stands in their way? (a grave epoch indeed).

But it may be said, "This is a great way off, in the extremest parts of the world; what is that to us?" If it be nothing to you, let it be nothing to you; I have told you it is somewhat to you.

It concerns all your religions and all the good interests of England.

I have, I thank God, considered, and I would beg of you to consider a little with me: what that resistance is that is likely to be made to this mighty current, which seems to be coming from all parts upon all Protestants; who is there that holdeth up his head to oppose this danger? A poor Prince (Charles X., King of Sweden, at present attacked by the King of Denmark; the Dutch also aiming at him), indeed poor; but a man in his person as gallant and truly I think I may say as good as any these last ages have brought forth; a man that hath adventured his all against the Popish interest in Poland and made his acquisition still good there for the Protestant religion. He is now reduced into a corner: and what addeth to the grief of all—more grievous than all that hath been spoken of before (I wish it may not be too truly said) is that men of our religion forget this, and seek his ruin (Dutch and Danes).

I beseech you consider a little: consider the consequences of all that! For what does it all signify? Is it only a noise? or hath it not withal an articulate sound in it? Men that are not true to the religion we profess—profess I am persuaded with greater truth, uprightness and sincerity than it is professed by any collected body, so nearly gathered together as these nations are in all the world. God will find them out (the low-minded Dutch, pettifogging for "Sound Dues," for "Possession of the Sound" and mere shopkeeper lucre). I beseech you consider how things do cooperate. Consider if this may seem but design against your well-being. It is a design against your very being; this artifice, and this complete design against the Protestant interest—wherein so many Protestants are not so right as were to be wished. If they can shut us out of the Baltic Sea and make themselves masters of that, where is your trade?......where will you be able to challenge any right by sea, or justify yourselves against a foreign invasion in your own soil? Think upon it! This is in design. I believe, if you will go and ask the poor mariner in his red cap and coat as he passeth from ship to ship you will hardly find in any ship but they will tell you this is designed against you. So obvious is it, by this and other things that you are the object, and in my conscience I know not for what else you are so but because of the purity of the profession amongst you; who have not yet made it your trade to prefer your profit before your godliness (whatever certain Dutch and Danes may do) but reckon godliness the greater gain. But should it happen, as contrivances stand, you should not be able to vindicate yourselves against all whomsoever—I name no one State upon this head—(do not name the Dutch with their pettifoggings for the Sound; no!) but I think all acknowledged States are engaged in the combination—judge you where you have accounted yourselves happy in being environed with a great ditch from all the world beside. Truly you will not be able to keep your ditch nor your shipping unless you turn your ships and shipping into troops of horse and companies of foot; and fight to defend yourselves on *terra firma*.

And these things stated, I have delivered my soul, and if there be "no danger" in all this I am satisfied. I have told you; you will judge if no danger! If you shall think we may have discourse of all things at pleasure (Carlyle—Debate for days and weeks, whether it shall be "House of Lords" or

" other House," put the question, Whether this question shall
be put and say ay, say no; and thrash the air with idle
jargon!) and that it is a time of sleep and ease and rest, without any due sense of these things—I have this comfort towards
God, I have told you of it. (Carlyle, Yes, your Highness! O
intemperate vain Sir Arthur, peppery Thomas Scott and ye
other constitutional Patriots, is there no sense of truth in you
then; no discernment of what really is what? Instead of
belief and insight, have you nothing but whirlpools of old
paper-clippings and a gray waste of Parliamentary constitutional logic?)

Really, were it not that France (give me leave to say it)
is a balance against that Party at this time!—Should there
be a Peace made (which hath been, and is still laboured and
aimed at, a general peace) then will England be the general
object of all the fury and wrath of all the enemies of God
and our religion in the world! I have nobody to accuse; but
do look on the other side of the water! You have neighbours
there, some that you are in amity with, some that have professed
malice enough against you. I think you are fully satisfied in
that. I had rather you would trust your enemy than some
friends, that is, rather believe your enemy and trust him that he
means your ruin, than have confidence in some who perhaps
may be in some alliance with you. (We have watched the
Dutch and their dealings in the Baltic lately!)—I perhaps
could enforce all this with some particulars, nay I certainly
could. For you know that your enemies be the same who
have been accounted your enemies ever since Queen Elizabeth
came to the Crown.

An avowed designed enemy all along, wanting nothing of
counsel, wisdom and prudence to root you out from the face
of the earth: (This was the design of that Catholic Rome,
with whom an immense body of our Clergy are coquetting,
calling their Church a branch of the Catholic, i.e. Roman
Catholic, Faith) and when public attempts (Spanish Armadas
and such like) would not do, how have they by the Jesuits

P.   2

and their other emissaries, laid foundations to perplex and
trouble our Government by taking away the lives of them
whom they judged to be of any use for preserving our peace!
(no mistake about their enmity). (Carlyle—Guy Faux and
Jesuit Garnett were a pair of pretty men; to go no farther.
Ravaillac in the Rue de la Ferronerie, and Stadtholder
Williams' Jesuit; and the night of St Bartholomew; here and
elsewhere they have not wanted "counsel" of a sort!) And
at this time I ask you, whether you do not think they are
designing, as busily as ever any people were, to prosecute the
same counsels and things to the uttermost?

The business then was: The Dutch needed Queen Elizabeth of famous memory for their protection. They had it,
had protection from her. I hope they will never ill requite it!
For if they should forget either the kindness that was then
shown them (which was their real safety) or the desires this
nation hath had to be at peace with them—truly I believe
whoever exercises any ingratitude in this sort will hardly
prosper in it. (Carlyle—He cannot, your Highness, unless God
and His Truth be a mere hearsay of the market, he never can.)

But this may awaken you, howsoever—I hope you will be
awakened upon all these considerations. It is certain they
(these Dutch) have professed a principle which, thanks be to
God, we never knew. They will sell arms to their enemies
and lend their ships to their enemies. They will do so. And
truly that principle is not a matter of dispute at this time;
"we are not here to argue with them about it," only let
everything weigh with your spirits as it ought. And we
must tell you, we do know that this of their having such a
principle is true. I dare assure you of it; and I think if but
your Exchange here in London were resorted to, it would let
you know, as clearly as you can desire to know, that they
have hired—sloops I think they call them, or some other name
—they have "let sloops on hire" to transport upon you
four-thousand foot and a thousand horse upon the pretended interest of that young man that was the late king's

son (what a designation for "Charles by the Grace of God"!),
and this is, I think, a thing far from being reckonable as a
suggestion to any ill end or purpose, a thing to no other end
than that it may awaken you to a just consideration of your
danger, and to uniting for a just and natural defence.

Indeed I never did, I hope I never shall, use any artifice
with you to pray you to help us with money for defending
ourselves, but if money be needful, I will tell you "Pray
help us with money that the interest of the nation may be
defended abroad and at home." I will use no arguments;
and thereby will disappoint the artifice of bad men abroad
who say, "It is for money." (They say so now.)

If this be the condition of your affairs abroad, I pray a
little consider what is the estate of your affairs at home, and
if both these considerations of home affairs and foreign have
but this effect, to get a consideration among you, a due and
just consideration; let God move your hearts for the answering of everything that shall be due unto the nation, as He
shall please. And I hope I shall not be solicitous; I shall
look up to Him who hath been my God and my Guide
hitherto. I say, I beseech you, look to your own affairs at
home, how they stand; I am persuaded you are all, I
apprehend you are all, honest and worthy good men, and
that there is not a man of you but would desire to be found
a good patriot. I know you would; we are apt to boast
sometimes that we are Englishmen: and truly it is no shame
for us that we are Englishmen, but it is a motive to us to do
like Englishmen and seek the real good of this nation and
the interest of it.......(This was a real Englishman.)

...It is through a wonderful, admirable and never to be
sufficiently admired providence of God that we are still in
peace; and the fighting we have had and the success we have
had—yea, we that are here, we are an astonishment to the
world......(so we are now, especially after the strategy of
Colenso, Spion Kop and Magersfontein). And take us in

that temper we are in, or rather in that distemper, it is the greatest miracle that ever befell the sons of men that we are got again to peace. And whoever shall seek to break it, God Almighty root that man out of this nation ; and He will do it, let the pretences be what they may !

Peace-breakers, do they consider what it is they are driving towards? They should do it ! He that considereth not the woman with child, the sucking children of this nation that know not the right hand from the left, of whom, for aught I know, it may be said this city is as full as Nineveh was, he that considereth not these must have the heart of Cain. (There is point in the remarks of this philanthropist !) For the wrath and justice of God will prosecute such a man to his grave, if not to hell. (Carlyle—Where is Sam Cooper or some "prince of limners" to take us that look of His Highness? I would give my ten best historical paintings for it, gilt frames and twaddle criticisms into the bargain.)

What is that which possesseth every sect ? What is it ? That every sect may be uppermost, and, I beseech you, judge what such a company of men of these sects are doing, while they are contesting one with another. They are contesting in the midst of a generation of men (a malignant episcopal party, I mean), contesting in the midst of these all united. What must be the issue of such a thing as this ? Some of the Cavaliers have invited the Spaniard himself to carry on the Cavalier cause.

...What is your defence? What hindereth the irruption of all this upon you, to your utter destruction ? Truly that you have an army.—And what is the case of your army withal? a poor unpaid army ; the soldiers going barefoot at this time, in this weather (Jan. 25th). And yet a peaceable people, these soldiers, seeking to serve you with their lives ; judging their pains and hazards and all well bestowed in obeying their officers and serving you, to keep the peace of these nations ! yea he must be a man with a heart as hard as the weather who hath not a due sense of this !

I say, judge what the state of Ireland will be if free-quarter for the army come upon the Irish people. You have a company of Scots in the north of Ireland (forty or fifty thousand of them settled there) who, I hope, are honest men (present day Orangemen).......And should the soldiers run upon free-quarter in your English Settlements in Ireland, the English planters must quit the country through their beggary and that which hath been the success of so much blood and treasure, to get that country into your hands, what can become of it, but that the English must needs run away for pure beggary, and the Irish must possess the country again for a receptacle to the Spanish interest? And hath Scotland been long settled? In good earnest I do think the Scots nation have been under as great a suffering in point of livelihood and subsistence outwardly as any people I have yet named to you. I do think truly they are a very ruined nation. *And yet in a way hopeful enough.* The meaner sort in Scotland live as well and are likely to come into as thriving a condition under your Government as when they were under their own great Lords who made them work for their living *no better than the peasants of France.* (Cromwell knew the state of France.) The middle sort of people do grow up there into such a substance as makes their lives comfortable if not better than they were before. (Carlyle— Scotland is prospering, has fair play and ready money; prospering, though sulky.)

If now, after all this, we shall not be sensible of all those designs that are in the midst of us : of the united Cavaliers ; of the designs which are animated every day from Flanders and Spain; while we have to look upon ourselves as a divided people. (Sentence off.)—A man cannot certainly tell where to find consistency anywhere in England.......How can any man lay his hand on his heart and permit himself to talk of things (" Roots of Constitutional Government," " Other House," " House of Lords " and such like) neither to be made out by the light of Scripture nor of reason ; and draw one another off from considering of these things (which are very palpable things)? I dare leave them with you and commit them to your bosom. They have a weight—a greater weight than any I have yet suggested to you, from abroad or at home. If such be our case abroad and at home, that our being and well-being—our well-being is not worth the naming comparatively—I say, if such be our case, of our being at home and abroad, that *through want to bear up our honour at sea and through want to maintain what is our defence at home we stand exposed to such dangers*; if through mistake we shall be led off from the consideration of these things ; and talk of circumstantial things, and *quarrel about circumstances* ; and shall not with heart and soul intend and carry on these things, I confess I can look for nothing other, I can say no other than what a foolish book expresseth of one that having consulted everything, could hold to nothing neither Fifth Monarchy, Presbytery nor Independency, nothing ; but at length concludes he is for nothing but an " orderly confusion " (not out of date for 1901).

...And now having said this I have discharged my duty to God and to you, in making this demonstration—and I profess not as a rhetorician ! My business was to prove the verity of the designs from abroad and the still unsatisfied spirits of the Cavaliers at home.

And I say if this be the truth I pray God affect your hearts with a due sense of it ! and give you one heart and mind to carry on this work for which we are met together !... We have had now six years of peace, and have had an interruption of ten years war. We have seen and heard and felt the evils of war. Shall we now be prodigal of time ? Should any man, shall we listen to delusions to break and interrupt this peace ?...Let us have one heart and soul ; one mind to maintain the honest and just rights of this nation ; not to pretend to them, to the destruction of our peace, to the destruction of the nation. (Carlyle—As yet there is one hero-heart among the blustering rabble, one soul blazing as a light-beacon in the midst of chaos, for-

bidding chaos yet to be supreme. In a little while that too
will be extinct; and then?) Really, pretend what we will,
if you run into another flood of blood and war, the sinews of
this nation being wasted by the last, it must sink and perish
utterly. (Note this, all ye that listen to the syren voice of
Brummagem Joe, threatening the French with war over mere
newspaper cartoons—over nothing.) I shall conclude with
this. I was free, the last time of our meeting, to tell you
I would discourse upon a Psalm, and I did it. I am not
ashamed of it at any time. (Carlyle—Why should you be,
your Highness? A word that does speak to us from the
eternal heart of things, "word of God" as you well call it, is
highly worth discoursing upon.) There you have one verse
which I forgot...."Let the people not return again to folly."
Indeed if we return again to folly, let every man consider, if
it be not like turning to destruction? If God shall unite your
hearts and bless you, and give you the blessing of union and
love one to another; and tread down everything that riseth
up in your hearts and tendeth to deceive your own souls with
pretences of this thing or that, as we have been saying
(sentence turns off)—and not prefer the keeping of peace
that we may see the fruit of righteousness in them that love
peace and embrace peace—it will be said of this poor nation,
Actum est de Anglia. It is all over with England!

But I trust God will never leave it to such a spirit. And
while I live and am able I shall be ready.—(Carlyle—Courage,
my brave one! Thou hast but some seven months more of it,
and then the ugly coil is all over; and thy part in it manfully
done; manfully and fruitfully to all eternity! Peppery Scott's
hot head can mount to Temple Bar, whither it is bound; and
England, with immense expenditure of liquor and tar barrels,
can call in its Nell-Gwyn Defender of the Faith—and make
out a very notable two-hundred years under *his* guidance and
finding itself now nearly got to the devil, may perhaps pause
and recoil and remember: who knows? Oliver is honourably
quit of it, he for one; and the Supreme Powers will guide it

farther according to their pleasure.) (Modern editor's query on this—*How about a Jersey Lily Defender?*) I shall be ready to stand and fall with you. I have taken my oath to govern "according to the laws" that are now made; and I trust I shall fully answer it. And know, I sought not this place (Carlyle—Who would have sought it that could have as nobly avoided it? Very scurvy creatures only. The "place" is no great thing I think—with either Heaven or else Hell so close upon the rear of it, a man might do without the "place." Know all men, Oliver Cromwell did not seek this place, but was sought to it, and led and driven to it by the necessities, the Divine Providences, the eternal Laws), I speak it before God, Angels and men : I did not. You sought me for it, you brought me to it; and I took my oath to be faithful to the interest of these nations, to be faithful to the Government... and so having declared my heart and mind to you in this I have nothing to say, but to pray, God Almighty bless you.

Thus ends this truly remarkable speech of one who clearly believed that words were given to man to express and not to conceal his feelings. We have already alluded to the power of Carlyle's comments in his *Cromwell*. Among the works of men of strong literary genius it usually happens that one of their productions stands out in marked superiority to the rest, and in our judgment Carlyle is no exception to this rule. Except for some passages in *Past and Present* we believe that his *Cromwell* marks the highest point of his genius, and that the most sublime and significant things that he ever wrote are contained therein. The Carlyle of the *Cromwell* and the Carlyle of *Frederick the Second* are two very different people. It is in a different strain that he records Voltaire's jests on the King's hæmorrhoids and labours to convince us that the canting, drunken old father of his hero who so foully did the poor boy Von Katte to death was really a *dumb poet*, and that he laughs away such matters as his hero's conduct over the Silesian Loan, etc., etc. This was the Carlyle of *The Nigger Question* and not of the *Cromwell*. Some of the passages of the latter display a sublime elevation of mind such as is contained in the *Upanishads*. We will conclude with one most luminous passage from his *Latter-Day Pamphlets* (No. 5, Stump Orator). It has recently fallen to the lot of the nation to read (in the "Manchester Speeches" and elsewhere) the candid and ingenuous accounts of the Balfours and the Lansdownes of their great surprise at finding that the Boers knew how to ride horses and to fight. It has also contemplated the spectacle of thousands of luckless privates festering away into their graves from the enteric, which the supply of even such a simple thing as a pocket filter by the Government (*vide* Conan Doyle) would often have prevented. Let us then listen to Carlyle ;

"The dog that was drowned last summer, and that floats up and down the Thames with ebb and flood ever since—is it not dead? Alas, in the hot months, you meet here and there such a floating dog; and at length if you often use the river steamers, get to know him by sight. 'There he is again, still astir there in his quasi-stygian element!' you dejectedly exclaim (perhaps reading your Morning Newspaper at the moment); and reflect, with a painful oppression of nose and imagination, on certain completed professors of parliamentary eloquence in modern times. Dead long since, but *not* resting ; daily doing motions in that Westminster region still—daily from Vauxhall to Blackfriars, and back again ; and cannot get away at all ! Daily (from Newspaper or river steamer) you may see him at some point of his fated course, hovering in the eddies, stranded in the ooze, or rapidly progressing with flood or ebb ; and daily the odour of him is getting more intolerable ; daily the condition of him appeals more tragically to gods and men."

NEUTRAL TRADE IN ARMS
AND SHIPS.

THE present attitude of the Government of this country,
when in a position of neutrality, to the commercial
transactions of its subjects in the way of supplying combatant
nations with the nerves and sinews of war, may be summarily
described by a quotation from the late Lord Palmerston. By
replying, "Catch them if you can," to the remonstrances of a
belligerent Government against the license with which British
subjects are allowed to carry on this trade, the noble lord
epigrammatically described the attitude of his country on this
subject. In other words, the English trader is unrestrained
by the Government from supplying either belligerent with
weapons to carry on the struggle, and his contraband
contracts are even treated as legal in the English Courts,
but if he should be caught by the injured party, the State
abandons him to his fate.

In this essay we propose to consider whether a continuance of this attitude in reality embraces the whole duty
of a neutral Government from the standpoint of the comity
of nations, and whether it is an attitude which is at all
consistent with our dignity or our conduct in certain other
international matters. The position among contraband

articles which is filled by arms and munitions of war with regard to their effect on an existing war is so unique and so different from that of any other contraband article (with one exception, to be mentioned later), that we shall confine ourselves in this essay mainly to the international questions which arise from this branch of contraband trade alone.

In every modern war the question has cropped up as a root of bitterness between belligerents and neutrals with ever-increasing intensity. It was so in 1854, in 1861, and in 1870, for reasons which are sufficiently obvious. "If," said Lord Grenville, "I have wrested my enemy's sword from his hands, the bystander who furnishes him with a fresh weapon can have no pretence to be considered as a neutral in the contest[1]."

Inasmuch as it is now fully recognized that the neutrality of a State, in order to be genuine, must be perfectly colourless in the eyes of both parties, it is now a well-settled point of international practice that a neutral *Government* is bound to abstain from furnishing supplies of this kind to a belligerent, whether in the way of commerce or otherwise. The United States, it is true, provided a glaring instance of a breach of this rule in 1870, in supplying the French with arms from their public arsenals; but their isolated position away from the company of European States has unfortunately rendered them frequently indifferent to the practice of European States in such matters. Moreover, the obloquy which this veritable scandal drew down on the offending nation sufficed to shew the strength of international opinion against the practice. Now, if it be conceded that supplies of this kind are illegal if furnished by a neutral *State*, it is hard

---

[1] Since the first publication of this essay (January 1899) the Boer War has occurred. The people of this country have now, we believe, learned by bitter experience of the use which the Boers made of Delagoa Bay as a base of supplies, that this question of neutral supplies of munitions of war is worthy of discussion.

to see wherein the case differs when they are furnished by the subjects of a neutral State.

Lord Cockburn, whose whole argument before the Geneva Arbitration was aimed against the existence of State responsibility for such acts, was fain to admit that "whatever obligations attach by the general principles of the law of nations to the State or community as a whole, are equally binding on its subjects or citizens. For the State or community is but the aggregate of its individual members, and what is forbidden to the entire body by that law is equally forbidden to its component parts. The State is bound to restrain its individual members from violating obligations which as a whole it is bound to fulfil."

In this country the State has so far embodied this view of its duties in its practice that a subject acts contrary to its municipal laws who (while the State is in a position of neutrality)—

(1) Supplies a belligerent with loans of money or with arms or munitions of war, if such supplies are made gratuitously (*animo adjuvandi*), and not in the course of trade (*De Wütz* v. *Hendricks*).

(2) Gives a belligerent the benefit of his personal services, whether gratuitously or not (Foreign Enlistment Act).

(3) Builds or equips a ship of war for a belligerent, whether as a trade transaction or otherwise (Foreign Enlistment Act).

It is only when we come to the question of the trade in arms and munitions of war carried on by *neutral subjects* with a belligerent State, that we find ourselves surrounded by a thick jungle of tangled verbiage and obscure phraseology, which serves to conceal the real principle of the matter from our gaze. Immense financial interests have so well watered and manured this jungle, and the sun of Mammon has shone encouragingly on it for so long, that its luxuriant vegetation almost hides the light of truth from the whole question. If the neutral subject be allowed to supply a belligerent with arms and munitions without let or hindrance from his State, why, it may be asked, has the legislature of this country so stringently forbidden its subjects from engaging, when neutral, in the trade in vessels of war with belligerent States, since a vessel of war is in fact, as Lord Stowell said, " a contraband article of the most noxious kind, but nevertheless only a contraband article " ? The answer to this inquiry is to be found in the rough facts of the war of 1861, and of the *Alabama* controversy.

The sale of ships of war to a belligerent by a neutral subject unhindered by the neutral Government, turned out in practice to be a complete *reductio ad absurdum* of the theory that the State has nothing to do with the private commercial dealings of its subjects in contraband. It was recognized, when too late, that to deny any responsibility to restrain acts of commerce which supplied one belligerent with its whole fighting navy after the war had begun, was to reduce the neutrality of the State to an absolute farce. Accordingly the Government forbade the departure of other war vessels of the *Alabama* type (such as the *Alexandra* and the *Pampero*) from their ports, they expended £110,000 on the purchase of certain gunboats (said to be intended for the Emperor of China), in case they should fall into the hands of one of the belligerents, and finally they made a forced purchase of two iron-clad rams which were being constructed by a Birkenhead firm for the insurgents.

In spite of these energetic acts, we do not find that any hindrance or obstacle, even of a negative kind, was put in the way of the gunmakers of this country who armed over a million men with rifles and muskets in the course of that war, although the precise difference in principle between supplying a belligerent with a couple of steel rams (for arming his ships) and supplying him with arms for his troops is hard to discover. If the State interferes in the one case in order to preserve its neutrality, it is surely bound to show at least a negative disapproval in the other by treating the trade as illegal in its courts. If the rifles had been supplied gratuitously to the combatants by well-wishers in this country, they would have committed an illegal act. Yet the mere fact that a few private persons realized immense fortunes thereby is sufficient to alter the quality of the act, although no one will question the fact that its effect on the war is the same in either case. It is the alchemy of gold, purely and simply, which transforms the nature of this unlawful trade in the eye of the legislature.

We have previously alluded to the jungle of loose phraseology in the existing literature on this subject, and we suggest that the source of all the confusion may be found in the utterances of one or two famous jurists whose reputation and position have combined to give authority to their utterances.

Lord Cockburn, in the course of his dissenting judgment at Geneva on the *Alabama* claims, alluded as follows to the question of contraband trade :—

"The right of the belligerent to intercept this species of commerce and the liability of the neutral to have his property captured and confiscated under such circumstances do not arise out of obligations inherent in the nature of neutrality. They are purely conventional, and, as it were, a compromise between the *power* of belligerents and the *rights* of neutrals." What shall we say of such "rights" as these ? If the neutral trader is really exercising a right, why should his Government (often far more powerful than the belligerent Government) always leave him to his fate ? Why should it allow any compromise between his *rights* and the *power* of the belligerent, without even a single diplomatic assertion of those rights ? The fact is that the neutral Government abandons the trader to the consequences of his hostile and unneutral acts as a sort of sop to Cerberus for the breach of its own neutrality, which has been committed under its very eyes from its own ports and with its own tacit acquiescence, for "he is on the side of the enemy who supplies him with the necessaries of war."

The language of the great American jurist, Chancellor Kent, on the same subject, betrays so similar a confusion of idea as to forcibly suggest the conclusion that the atmosphere of glorious uncertainty, the freedom from binding authority, and the lack of agreement among the text writers which pervade the study of international law, produce a kind of vertigo of the mind on these powerful intellects hitherto restrained by the iron fetters of statute and precedent. "The *right* of the neutral," he says, "to transport (contraband to one of the belligerents) and of the hostile power to seize are *conflicting rights*, and neither party can charge the other with a criminal act."

What is the ethical or the legal meaning of the word "right" in this passage? We are told that one party has a "right" to do a certain act which vitally damages another with whom he has no quarrel, and that the other party has a "conflicting right" to stop him.

It should be noted that this dictum of the famous Chancellor has been uniformly treated as Biblical and quoted and relied upon as a model of inspired wisdom by the host of lesser writers including "Historians" whose opinions are always "mortised and adjoined" to those of the great. The passage may be appropriately interpreted as follows :—"The *right* of Red Indian A to take the scalp of Red Indian B, and the right of Red Indian B to stop him if he can, are *conflicting rights*, and neither party can charge the other with a criminal act." In the present case the neutral and the belligerent are in a state of peace *inter se* which shows up the monstrous farce of talking about "rights" in connection with such inimical acts. A further comment on these so-called "conflicting rights" is furnished by the fact that every Treaty of Navigation and Commerce entered into between the maritime powers, from the Treaty of Munster, in 1648, to our own day, with one solitary exception, contains a reservation against the trade in and the transport of contraband. Moreover, at the convention of maritime powers known as the "Second Armed Neutrality," which was held in the year 1800, with the express object of stretching the rights of neutral traders to the uttermost, the representatives of the various powers agreed in declaring the carriage of contraband to be illegal. During the American War of Independence, Lord Stormont at Paris, and Sir Joseph Yorke at the Hague, were instructed to utter repeated complaints against the trade in munitions of war between North America and France and Holland, and the Dutch Government in particular were informed that "His Majesty expects that their High Mightinesses will take measures, without delay, to stop the despatch of munitions of war by any means, direct or indirect, to North America," and they accordingly did stop it. Yet, in the face of such facts as these, we are gravely told by the highest authorities, that the traffic is not wrong, and that the neutral trader even has a "conflicting right" to carry it on.

The late Mr W. E. Hall, the greatest of English publicists, according to his wont is frankly utilitarian on this point. "Acts done even with intent to injure a foreign State are only wrong in so far as they compromise the nation of which the individual is a member. It (contraband traffic) is prevented (by the injured belligerent), because it is inconvenient, *not because it is a wrong*, and to allow the performance by a subject of an act not in itself improper cannot constitute a crime on the part of the State to which he belongs" (*International Law*, p. 80). Beyond this dogmatic statement of his views Mr Hall does not attempt to deal with the ethical aspect of a trade which put arms into the hands of a million men in the course of a modern war, and turned this country, professedly a neutral, into the arsenal of a belligerent nation.

On the face of it, the trade would appear to be "not wrong" in Mr Hall's opinion, on the same ethical grounds on which Chancellor Kent bases his "rights."

At the root of the matter lie the two opposite conceptions of the basis of the international duty of a neutral State, between which there is a great gulf fixed. So great is that gulf, that the writings of every publicist and the acts of every statesman are leavened according as he holds one or other of these views of the standard by which international conduct should be guided. The first of these opposing conceptions may be well illustrated by some remarks by Professor Westlake on this very subject of State interference in contraband trade carried on by subjects of a neutral State. Writing in the *Revue de Droit International* (vol. 2), the Professor asks, "Why is a belligerent not allowed to seize neutral commerce except under conditions which determine the contraband character (of the goods)? Simply because experience has shown that these conditions form the limit of the degree of intervention that neutrals would tolerate."

Later on he says, "The *law* rests at the point where the pretensions of belligerents and the resistance of neutrals are in equilibrium." And Mr W. E. Hall, writing on the same subject, says, as we have seen, that "Acts done, even with intent to injure a foreign State, are only *wrong* in so far as they compromise the nation of which the individual is a member." Lord Cockburn says, "The other party looks on the existing restraints on the freedom of neutral commerce as encroachments on his *rights*, and considering these restraints as arising entirely from convention, denies the illegality of any trade which the actual practice of nations does not prevent."

These extracts have one feature in common. They all deny, by implication, that International Law rests on a moral basis. Mr Westlake treats the dread of violence like a barometer, by consulting which the exact measure of neutral "rights" and "duties" may be ascertained. Mr Hall appears to gauge the moral quality of the act of the neutral trader by the amount of "fuss" which the injured State is likely to make.

It will be noticed that Lord Cockburn, who identified himself with the opinions of "the other party," sets up the actual practice of nations as the guide for international conduct in this matter, and considers existing restraints on the trade as an encroachment on the rights of the neutral trader. We have already pointed out that if the so-called rights of the trader had the least scintilla of right about them, no encroachment of them would be passively tolerated by the neutral Government.

The question as to how far the actual practice of nations is a satisfactory guide for international conduct is well illustrated by a quotation from the British *Case* at the Geneva Arbitration. On page 12 it is there said, "The British Government believes that the arbitrators would search in vain...in the general practice of maritime nations, for any proof of a duty incumbent on neutral Governments to prevent their subjects from supplying belligerents with ships adapted to warlike use, nor would they find any distinction drawn in this respect between the sale and delivery of a vessel built to order and that of a vessel not built to order." Chancellor Kent was even of opinion that the practice of nations allowed a neutral Government to supply troops under treaty, to a belligerent, without thereby forfeiting its neutrality. Moreover, the actual practice of States did not forbid the supply of coal to a war-vessel in neutral ports before the war of 1861. In all these cases it is evident that this test of international obligation is valueless to a State which wishes to fulfil its duties honourably.

The other view of the basis of international duty is founded on the great conception that States have a moral sense, like individuals in a civilized community, and as such have duties to one another which arise solely from the possession of that sense, and have no reference whatever to any "fear of violent retaliation."

The submission of the celebrated *Alabama* Claims to arbitration by Great Britain was an attempt, generous but unfortunate, by this country, to do its duty as a member of the company of States, towards the other members, without any reference to the fear or the expediency which the cynic and the utilitarian discover in all international actions.

It is now recognized that a State in the position of a neutral should not only itself abstain from tendering any help whatever to either of two belligerents, but, further, should do its best to restrain its subjects from doing the like. It was in this spirit that the last Foreign Enlistment Act of 1871 was framed. The Royal Commissioners in 1868, on the results of whose labours the Act was framed, said, "We have not felt ourselves bound to consider whether we were exceeding what could actually be required by international law, but we are of opinion that if those recommendations should be adopted, the municipal law of this realm available for the enforcement of neutrality will acquire increased efficiency, and will, so far as we can see, have been brought into full conformity with your Majesty's international obligations." The Act itself, as we have before stated, gives effect to the sense of responsibility for the acts of its subjects which the war of 1861 so clearly brought home to this country, especially as regards the building or equipping of ships of war in the course of trade, for belligerents, or supplying them with coal, or enlisting in their service.

If it is no part of the duty of a neutral State to place any restraint on its subjects' dealings in arms and munitions with a belligerent, it is surely not concerned with the way in which the subject disposes of his services. Yet the law, which forbids so stringently the departure of a single neutral recruit, offers no obstacle to the issue of unlimited supplies of arms and munitions to the belligerents.

If we turn, now, to the opinions of other text-writers on this subject, we find a succession of inconsistencies in their statements of a truly remarkable character. Bynkershoek, it is true, as a practical statesman, clearly gives his opinion that there is no difference in principle between supplying a belligerent with weapons and supplying him with men. If the one is allowed, then the other should be also. " Quod juris est," he says, " in instrumentis bellicis idem esse puto in militibus apud amicum populum comparandis." M. Bluntschli and M. Calvo, among modern writers, both seem to hesitate on the subject, and eventually deliver themselves of the opinion that large commercial dealings in arms and munitions of war, between a neutral subject and a belligerent, are unlawful, but that this is not so with small transactions, thereby forcibly recalling the argument of the young person in *Midshipman Easy*, who admitted the illegitimacy of her child, but pleaded that the offence was condoned because it was such a very little one.

The authors of the *Case for the United States*, at the Geneva Arbitration, draw the same distinction. They first (p. 84) " assert with confidence that a neutral ought not to permit a belligerent to use the neutral soil as the main, if not the only, base of its military supplies "; yet on the very next page, mindful of the fact that their fellow-citizens are the greatest sinners of all in the matter of contraband traffic, they are careful to allude to " the well-settled right of a neutral to manufacture and sell to either belligerent during a war, arms, munitions, and military supplies." If there be a " well-settled right " to sell such things, why should the quantity make any difference ? M. Calvo, it is true, subsequently prepared some *règles* for the general guidance of the nations of the world, in which the trade in arms, whether in large or small quantities, was prohibited ; but the value of the prohibition is somewhat damaged by the fact that it is coupled with a provision that in case of a blockade no ship should be liable to capture for attempting a breach of it until it should have been once warned by one of the blockading squadron, and an "annotation" of the fact placed on the ship's papers. This means that in future an intending blockade-runner (like the dog in English law, which was supposed to be allowed "one worry") would be enabled to make at least one clear attempt at breach of the blockade, with the unspeakable comfort of knowing that no worse thing could come upon him than an "annotation" on his ship's papers. Professor Westlake, in an article in the *Revue de Droit International* (vol. 2), after advocating the strong measure of making blockade-running a breach of municipal law, is of opinion, nevertheless, that the trade in arms and munitions of war is lawful for the subjects of a neutral country *provided they have dealt in them beforehand.* If the trade is lawful at all, the reason for this proviso is exceedingly obscure. A war creates an immense demand for a certain article of commerce, and a neutral trader undertakes to meet that demand. What conceivable difference can it make in the principle of the thing, whether he was in the habit of supplying that article beforehand or not? He is either free to trade in it or he is not.

M. Ortolan, a once celebrated French International lawyer, found a saving distinction between the sale of a ship of war by a neutral subject to a belligerent as a "ready-made" article of contraband and between building it to his order. The first he considers lawful, and the second unlawful, but the reasoning on which the difference rests does not appear.

Mr Lorimer (*Revue de Droit International*, vol. 2) adheres to "the grand principle of free exchange," and suggests that if the German Government had sold back to the French the arms captured at Sedan, they would thereby have themselves received the gains which later in the war found their way to the neutral traders of England and America, a most significant fact for the statesman and the economist of the future. M. Masse thinks that the goods only become contraband at the moment when they go out of the country in a direction where, by their nature, they are so, but not before. It is the frequent occurrence of statements of the foregoing description which has tended more than anything else to bring the great subject of International Law into ridicule with many logically-minded persons. The plain and vigorous language of Sir Robert Phillimore is in marked contrast to these confused utterances. " If the fountains of International Justice have been correctly pointed out in a former volume, and if it be the true character of a neutral to abstain from every act which may better or worsen the condition of a belligerent, the unlawfulness of any such trade is a necessary conclusion from these premises. What does it matter *where* the neutral supplies one belligerent with the means of attacking another? Is the cannon, or the sword, or the recruit who is to use them, less dangerous to the belligerent because they were purchased or he was enlisted within the limits of neutral territory? Surely the *locus in quo* is wholly beside the mark." The duties imposed on nations who wish to enjoy peace in the middle of the evils of war is not to put arms in the hands of either belligerent.

Turning now to the more solid arguments of the opponents of any interference by a neutral State in the export of arms and munitions by its subjects, we find that substantially they amount to four, viz.:—

(1) That neutrals have a right to follow their ordinary trades as in time of peace without reference to a war in which they have no concern.

(2) That it is impossible to define or limit the term " contraband " for the purpose of State interference, or to obtain general assent to any such definition among the nations.

(3) That any interference in such trade on the part of the State would create an intolerable burden of responsibility.

(4) That as long as a State has the money to pay for them, it has a right to purchase its arms and munitions where it pleases.

(1) The first argument has been so frequently reiterated by the great body of writers who uphold the existing state of things, that it requires to be dealt with at some length. It is usual among that body to rely on two Biblical statements of the case to justify the faith that is in them, so we proceed to set them out verbatim. "On what ground of reason or justice," said Lord Cockburn, "should their (neutral traders') right of *peaceful trade* be taken away, and their interests thus be damaged by reason of a war *in which they have no concern?*" In 1793 Mr Jefferson wrote: "Our citizens have always been free to make, vend, and export arms. It is the constant occupation of some of them. To suppress their callings because a war exists in foreign and distant countries *in which we have no concern*, would scarcely be expected. It would be hard in principle and impossible in practice. The law of nations, therefore, respecting the rights of those at peace, does not require from them such an internal derangement of their occupations."

In order to apprehend how little this traffic really has in common with any of the ordinary avocations of peace, and how far it should be protected from "derangement," it will suffice to quote the actual figures of that traffic (furnished by Professor Bernard in his *History of the Neutrality of Great Britain, etc.*) during the war of 1861, as between Great Britain and the United States, and Great Britain and the British West India Islands.

In 1860, before the war broke out, the value of the arms exported from this country to the United States amounted to £45,076. In 1862 the figures had risen to £999,197, but in

1866, after the end of the war, they had dropped to £82,345. The value of the same trade between Great Britain and the West Indies for the first of those years did not exceed £6050. In 1862, after Nassau had become a huge depôt for the supply of arms to the South, it had increased to £367,578, although in 1866 it again shrank to £4795.

Surely it is ridiculous to call this trade of putting arms into the hands of belligerents, after war has broken out, a continuance of the ordinary trade of peace in the face of figures which show in one case an increase of some 2000 per cent. in the value of the trade after the outbreak of war, and as sudden a shrinkage immediately the war is over. We have here truly a "derangement" in the trade, although of an opposite kind to that contemplated by Mr Jefferson.

The plain fact of the matter is that on such occasions the neutral country becomes the arsenal from which supplies are furnished, without which it would be impossible for one or other of the combatants to prolong the war. The trade then carried on by the neutral merchant is an adventitious one, which depends solely on the war for its creation and existence, and is absolutely different alike in its cause and its effect from an ordinary trade of peace.

(2) We come now to the question of the practical difficulty of defining or limiting the term contraband for the purpose of State interference in its export.

With regard to the proposal to limit the term for this purpose to "arms and objects directly used to wound," Professor Westlake (*Revue de Droit International*, vol. 2), after remarking that this proposal shows an attachment to "la forme matérielle et brute," worthy only of children or savages, continues, "It would be impossible to found a principle on the degree of utility of the article sold, or on the approximate degree to which it will be employed to actually kill and wound. International Law recognizes that no principle can be based on mere probabilities."

The quality of mind implied in this fixing of the gaze on "la forme matérielle et brute" is, nevertheless, the only one which is suitable for the settling of practical questions of this kind. In actual warfare on land the utility of arms and munitions is infinitely greater than that of any other article whatever, and we suggest that the mere probability that a rifle will be more serviceable than, *e.g.*, a flannel shirt is sufficiently great to found a principle for State interference. The fact that certain articles occasionally acquire an adventitious importance in warfare (as in the case of the famous barricade of biscuit tins) in no way affects the "mighty cleavage" which exists between arms and munitions of war and all other contraband articles whatever.

(3) As regards the question of the burden of International responsibility, which it is said would be incurred by the State with regard to the carrying out of any prohibition it might place on the export of arms, it should be observed that the measure of declaring all contracts of that kind void and unenforceable at law would entail no such responsibility, while the taint of illegality would deal a heavy blow at the trade, by driving the more cautious capitalists out of it. Even as regards actual intervention by the State, Great Britain has herself embodied the principle in various treaties, *e.g.* with Denmark in 1670 and 1780, with Russia in 1801, and with Spain in 1814, and in 1848 during the war between Prussia and Denmark the traffic in arms destined for the war was accordingly stopped.

Turning to the practice of Continental countries in the matter, M. Treitt thus stated the practice of France in 1867 for the benefit of the Neutrality Laws Commission: "Powder and war arms do not enjoy ordinary commercial freedom. These two objects are under the rigorous watch of the Government, and it is very difficult to arm a ship or even to load a cargo of powder or munitions of war without the Government hearing of it and being able to stop it." The

French Legislature has laid down most elaborate regulations on the subject, and a "permit" from the Minister of War is always required before exportation. Moreover, in 1870, from the outbreak of war, we find that Belgium, Holland, Switzerland, Austria, Denmark, Spain, and Italy, expressly prohibited, under penalties, the export to the belligerents of horses, arms, and munitions of war, and nothing happened afterwards which tended to show that the responsibility thereby incurred was excessive.

(4) The last argument with which we have to deal is usually stated as follows : " As long as either party to a contest has any resources left, it has a right to turn those resources into arms and munitions by means of neutral traders. The only condition imposed on the neutral is that he shall not refuse to one what he supplies to the other." The constant use of this argument among advocates of non-interference, coupled with assertions, that by enabling the parties to "fight it out," a "more lasting peace" is likely to result, appears to entitle it to serious discussion. It will suffice to point out that to enable a combatant to turn his resources into weapons at a particular time and place, is as vital an interference in the struggle as can well be imagined. It would be as reasonable to contend that the British were free to supply the Spaniards with a fighting fleet on the scene of action at Cuba, provided their resources in Europe were sufficient to pay for the ships. The one-sided nature of such aid was well shown in the Crimean War, when the supplies of the Germans and the Belgians, useless to the English, alone enabled Russia to prolong the struggle against the allies.

The recriminations on this subject which the British Government then addressed to the Germans and the Belgians, show that the eyes of the former were opened on that occasion, at least, in an unpleasantly practical way to the real nature of the traffic as has happened again over Delagoa Bay.

Moreover, traces are not wanting in recent years of the awakening of public opinion on the subject. Throughout the Franco-German War the trade was consistently denounced by certain journals, and on August 4, 1871, a resolution was even brought forward in the House of Commons with the object of prohibiting it. Lord Granville also intimated to Count Bismarck that his Government would be willing to enter into a conference with the other powers for the same object.

Professor Bernard has well said that, "between performing your duty impartially and violating it impartially, there is a most material difference. The belligerent has a right to have the law observed in his favour, and not broken in his favour. In such cases, indeed, equality is seldom equity."

In modern times the inconsistent behaviour of three great states (England, Prussia, and the United States), as regards the commercial dealings of its subjects in contraband, furnishes an excellent illustration of the need for a clear international agreement on the subject.

In 1854 remonstrances as stated above were addressed by the English to the Prussian Government against the supplies of arms, etc., which Prussian and Belgian subjects were constantly furnishing to the Russians in the Crimea. Thereupon the Prussians undertook to stop the Belgian supplies which were passing through their territory, but not those of their own countrymen.

In 1870, it was Prussia's turn to remonstrate with England concerning the supplies of arms by British subjects to the French. Count Bismarck contended that if the British arguments were well founded in 1854, the conduct of the Prussians on that occasion did not justify a breach of the principles for which the English then contended. They further contended that the sympathies of the British public were with the German and not with the French cause, and they excused their own conduct in 1854 on the ground that Russia was in the position of one power fighting against four.

The introduction into a discussion of this kind of matters relating to the sympathies of a neutral nation, or the justice of the war, is necessarily fatal to the discovery of the abstract truth of the matter.

The conduct of the United States manifested a similar inconsistency. In 1870, at the very time when the *Alabama* claims, whereby it was sought to extend the responsibility of a neutral state to an extent hitherto quite unknown, were being put forward with as much rhetoric as possible, we find that the Government threw open their arsenals for the benefit of the French, and that 96,000 rifles and 11,000,000 cartridges were sold by them and paid for through the French Consul. A more flagrant breach of International Law it would be hard to imagine.

The reasons for State interference in blockade-running are precisely similar to the reasons for interference in the branches of contraband trade with which we have dealt. The same question arises as to whether the financial interests of the few shall prevail over the interests of the nation in maintaining international good-feeling. If a nation connives at the acts of its subjects in defeating or rendering futile the war operations of a friendly State, it cannot complain if that State is aggrieved at the loss of an advantage which is often hardly earned, or if the recollection of such grievances continues to rankle after the war is over.

We proceed to quote once more from the facts of the war of 1861. The use of steam power and the freedom from State interference combined to develop blockade-running from British ports to the blockaded ports of the south into a flourishing industry. Professor Bernard, in his *History of the Neutrality of Great Britain*, p. 289, thus describes the state of things in that war: "One effect of the pressure of the blockade was to impart activity to blockade-running. As the first winter of the war passed away—as summer followed spring, and it became evident that both parties had strength and resolution for a long struggle—the temptations held out by this new field of mercantile adventure necessarily increased. British merchants entered it, and British capital flowed into it, by degrees. Cargoes were now despatched on the joint account of several speculators, each taking his share of profit and loss; or a vessel carried out at a high rate of freight the separate ventures of a number of individual shippers. The ships bound on these voyages were never advertised, nor was their destination publicly made known, and it is impossible to form anything like an estimate of the extent to which the traffic was really carried on, or the number of persons concerned in it. Of twenty steamers which are said to have been kept plying, in 1863, between Nassau and two of the blockaded ports, seven belonged to a firm at Charlestown, who had a branch house at Liverpool, and through whom the Confederate Government transacted its business in England. As the nature of the risks to be encountered, and the precautions to be observed became better known, vessels began to be built specially adapted for this purpose."

"In the Clyde, as I remember, any observer might have noticed in 1863 and 1864, more than one speedy and insidious-looking craft fitted for sea—long, very low, drawing little water, yet with considerable stowage, painted of a dull greenish-grey colour, with a short raking funnel, or pair of funnels, and nothing aloft to catch the eye. These were blockade-runners of the newest pattern."

Mr Adams, the American minister in London, in his letter of May 12, 1862, after alluding to the systematic plan to violate the blockade which existed in this country, continued as follows : "I doubt not your Lordship will see at a glance the embarrassment in which a country is necessarily involved, by complaints raised of the continued severity of the blockade by a friendly nation, which, at the same time, confesses its inability to restrain its subjects from stimulating the resistance that necessitates a continuance of the very state of things of which they make complaint."

The British port of Nassau in the Bahamas speedily became a sort of halfway house for running the blockade of the Confederate ports. "The harbour of Nassau, usually quiet and almost empty, was soon thronged with shipping of all kinds, and its wharves and warehouses became an entrepôt for cargoes brought thither from different quarters. Agents of the Confederate Government resided there, and were busily employed in assisting and developing the traffic."

It was through this essentially non-neutral use of a British port that the Federal Government was driven, in self-defence, to make use of the theory of "continuous voyage," for the purpose of seizing cargoes nominally intended for Nassau, but really intended, after transhipment, for the blockaded ports.

We would not for one moment advocate recognition by a neutral of any mere paper blockade which a belligerent is pleased to declare, but what we do contend is, that if one belligerent has succeeded in establishing an actual blockade of the ports of another, it is the duty of a neutral Government to show something more than passive indifference if its own ports are used as a base of operations to defeat the purposes of the blockade. Inaction in such a case becomes complicity.

In the case of a land blockade of an enemy's town by military forces, no question ever arises as to the liberty of subjects of a neutral State to supply the inhabitants of the invested place with food or arms. It may, of course, be argued that this is so for the very good reason that to attempt to pass the enemy's lines would be absurd, but if we go on the supposition, for a moment, that it was possible during the siege of Paris for the provision dealers or gun-makers of England to supply the Parisians by means of some aerial contrivance with food and arms in sufficient abundance to enable them to hold out against the German forces, it will not be difficult to imagine the feelings of the German Government towards a neutral State in such a case, which was passively allowing its subjects to undo all the work on which the former were expending so much blood and treasure. The mere geographical accident that a town happens to be on the sea-coast cannot affect the principle which governs both cases. It is noteworthy that by the 15th Article of the Danish Maritime Code " no shipmaster shall sail to any port blockaded from the seaside by one of the belligerent powers, and he shall in every respect carefully pay attention and conform to the warnings communicated to him by the authorities relative to the blockade of ports."

By the 18th Article, breach of this regulation exposes the offender to the risk of forfeiting his right to Danish citizenship, and to prosecution by the tribunals of his country.

A brief consideration of the legality of supplying coal in neutral ports to belligerent war-vessels, throws a flood of light on the whole subject of contraband trade. All the arguments against State interference in the matter apply even more forcibly to the sale of coal than to the sale of arms. The export of coal is an " ordinary avocation of peace " with many persons in this country, and, therefore, " ought not to be interfered with by reason of a war in which they have no concern." Moreover, the strictest impartiality in freely supplying both sides could be confidently expected from traders, and no one will dispute the fact that it aids belligerent nations most materially to " fight out " their quarrels, while, lastly, its use for many peaceful purposes ought to preclude any interference in its export, since we have already been told, that it is impossible to found a principle on the degree of utility (to a belligerent) of the article sold, and that no principle can be rested on mere probabilities.

At the commencement of the war of 1861, there was no international practice against allowing belligerent war-vessels to coal freely in neutral ports, yet before the end of that war, and again in 1870, this country and the bulk of civilized States, with maritime ports, found it necessary, in order to preserve their neutrality, to make stringent regulations to the effect: (1) that no belligerent war-vessel should be allowed to coal at the same port twice within three months; (2) and that the supply afforded should be only sufficient to carry the vessel to the nearest port. The reason for these regulations is thus lucidly stated by the late Mr Hall (*International Law*, p. 630): "To permit more to be obtained than can in a reasonably liberal sense of the word be called necessary for reaching a place of safety, is to provide the belligerent with means of aggressive action, and *consequently to violate the essential principles of neutrality*." Elsewhere he says, that *a war-vessel if allowed to coal freely in neutral ports obtains as solid an advantage as Russia in a war with France would derive from being allowed to march her troops across Germany*, for she would be enabled to reach her enemy at a spot which would otherwise be unattainable. It is strange that a writer, with such clear views on this subject, should have no word to say against the conduct of the Germans in the last war between Russia and France in supplying the former with the means of aggression *ad libitum* in the shape of arms and shot and shell. The reason why the State had to interfere in the case of coal supplies is to be found in the fact that in that case the effects of the breach of neutrality committed by the neutral trader are almost immediately made manifest by the depredations of the cruisers, whereas the effects of the supply of arms, though often as far reaching, are not so clearly perceptible. The usual method among text-writers for explaining away the incongruity existing in international conduct over these two cases, consists in making use of verbiage to the effect that a neutral country must not become the "base of operations" for the "armed expeditions of a belligerent," and the interference with the "liberty of the subject to trade" in coal, or in ships of war with a belligerent, is explained to their satisfaction by this phrase. Now, if a ship of war is an important part of an "armed expedition," and, therefore, not a fit object of commerce, we submit that a million rifles, and a corresponding amount of ammunition, may also be an important part of an armed expedition, and that the country which supplies them is as truly a base of operations as if it supplied war-vessels, and therefore that the alleged distinction is an imaginary one. As food is to the human body, so is coal to the war-vessel, and so are munitions of war to the belligerent.

We find it necessary to make some allusion here to an essay on neutral trade in contraband of war, published nearly forty years ago by a certain politician under the name of "Historicus." We should have avoided all reference to it but for the fact that the erudition and political eminence of the author have caused the essay to be still regarded as an authority on the subject. Moreover, the learned author has not, to the best of our belief, ever contradicted the views he has therein expressed.

The essay is chiefly filled with declamation of a very florid description against the views we have here been advocating. "We have the misfortune," exclaims the writer, "to live in days when in the name of liberalism, philanthropy, and civilization we are invited to upset the whole fabric of international law, which the *reason* of jurists has designed and the usage of nations has built up, and to rear upon its ruins the trumpery edifice of a shallow caprice. I would that we had yet among us the multitudinous eloquence of Burke, or the poignant wit of Canning, to do condign justice upon this

presumptuous sciolism." Poor M. Hautefeuille, who held
that neutral trade in contraband of war was unlawful, is
characterized, in consequence, as "without an equal, even in
the modern license of coxcombical jurisprudists." Then
the writer proceeds to make a number of "unhesitating assertions" to the effect that the doctrine of State interference
in such trade is contrary to the principles which all the
authorities have established, and which the universal practice
of nations has confirmed. "It is a discreditable thing to the
state of international science," he continues, "that it should
be necessary at the present time to cite authority in support
of propositions so elementary, and which ought to be beyond
the possibility of dispute." Elsewhere he alludes to the
doctrine as a "new-fangled monstrosity," "the bantling of
the Abbé Galiani," and the "unauthorised crotchet of M.
Hautefeuille," and he quotes Wheaton's (*American*) opinion,
that the consideration of it was "an idle question," and "too
contemptible for discussion." The solemnity with which the
writer reproduces Chancellor Kent's well-worn fallacy about
"conflicting rights" is very impressive. "Permit me, while
I am warning your readers against *false lights*, to refer them
to a guide who will *never lead them astray*—to the greatest
jurist whom this age has produced. I mean the American
Chancellor Kent. Of his writings it may safely be said that
they are never wrong." The writer then expresses his
regret and astonishment that Dr Phillimore, so far from con-
demning this monstrosity, actually approves and adopts it.
"The only argument adduced by Dr Phillimore against the
well-established rule, is an appeal to the 'eternal principles
of justice.'......I can only express my confident hope that
in advising the Crown, the Queen's Advocate will have
regard rather to the law and practice of nations than to the
'principles of eternal justice,' which it should seem on this
subject are hardly compatible with reason and common sense."
After setting out verbatim all the well-known extracts from

the authorities which we have quoted previously, none of which touch the principle of the matter at all, the writer concludes with a fine piece of declamation. The italics are not in the original. "It is by the recognition of and obedience to fixed principles of *right*, that the society of nations is alone enabled to escape an incessant appeal to the last arbitrament of the sword. *Misera est servitus ubi jus incertum*. No wrong more serious or more indefensible can be wrought to the commonwealth of mankind than that which is committed by rash and inconsiderate writers who presume of their own caprice to discredit, to pervert, and to undermine the settled principles of public law. Like wreckers, they hang out deceptive beacons which lure the vessel of state upon the rocks.......It is of the last importance to eradicate from the public mind on both sides of the Atlantic these *pernicious errors*, on whatever authority they may be promulgated. The statement of M. Hautefeuille is a monstrous and mischievous solecism. If the reassertion of these principles, *founded in reason*, settled by law, consolidated by experience, *accepted by the unanimous accord of nations*, tends in any degree to remove that irritation which is the unhappy fruit of ignorance inflamed by passion, the object of this letter will have been accomplished." Thus ends the essay of "Historicus," which suggests by its contents the last comment of Macbeth on his own existence, viz. that it was full of sound and fury, signifying nothing.

If we inquire dispassionately in what the "deceptive beacons" consist, which are used, as "Historicus" asserts, by "wreckers," like Sir R. Phillimore, to lure the ship of state on the rocks, it will be found that they consist in the simple assertion that if two states are at war, and a third state claims all the privileges of neutrality, it ought to endeavour to restrain its subjects from a vital interference in the conflict by supplying the belligerents with weapons during the struggle. This proposition is so simple that we think it would outrage the sporting instincts of any fair-minded licensed victualler or pugilist if he were asked to assent to the contrary.

There is one other matter in connection with this subject which may, in the future, affect the interests of this country to an enormous extent. We have already alluded incidentally to the sale of ships of war to belligerents by neutral subjects. In spite of the deeds of the *Alabama,* in spite of the latest Foreign Enlistment Act, and in spite of the Geneva Arbitration, we still find a writer of the highest authority (the late Mr W. E. Hall), so recently as 1895, giving utterance to the following statement: " The direct logical conclusions to be obtained from the ground principles of neutrality go no further than to prohibit the issue from neutral waters of a vessel (1) provided with a belligerent commission, or (2) belonging to a belligerent, and able to inflict damage on the enemy."

" It is fully recognized," he says, " that a vessel completely armed and in every respect fitted, the moment it receives its crew to act as a man-of-war is a proper subject of commerce. There is nothing to prevent its neutral possessor from selling it and undertaking to deliver it to the belligerent either in the neutral port or in that of the purchaser, subject to the right of the other belligerent to seize it as contraband if he meets it on the high seas or within his enemy's waters. 'There is nothing,' says Mr Justice Story, 'in the law of nations that forbids our citizens from sending armed vessels as well as munitions of war to foreign ports for sale. It is a commercial adventure which no nation is bound to prohibit.' If the neutral may sell his vessel when built, he may build it to order.......It would appear, therefore, arguing from general principles alone, that a vessel of war may be built, armed, and furnished with a minimum navigating crew; and that in this state, provided it has not received a commission, it may clear from a neutral harbour on a confessed voyage to a belligerent port without any infraction of neutrality having been committed."

Mr Hall admits "that an international usage prohibiting the construction and outfit of vessels of war, in the strict sense of the term, is in course of growth; but that, although it is adopted by the most important maritime powers, it is not yet old enough or quite wide enough to have become compulsory on those nations which have not yet signified their voluntary adherence to it; but in the mean time a ship of war may be built and armed to the order of a belligerent and delivered to him outside neutral territory ready to receive a fighting crew, or it may be delivered to him within such territory, and may issue as belligerent property if it is neither commissioned nor so manned as to be able to commit immediate hostilities."

Now, if the "ground principles" of neutrality really authorised anything of the kind, the only observation we should make would be that the sooner the ground was shifted on which those principles rested, the better it would be. The papers contained in the "Report of the Neutrality Laws Commission" of the year 1868 provide us with a few facts which form a sufficiently ludicrous commentary on Mr Hall's "ground principles."

On April 15, 1863, the agents of the Southern States contracted with M. Arman, a private French shipbuilder, to build four steamers, which could be used as passenger-boats, but should be capable of mounting twelve pieces of cannon. On July 15 two more vessels of the same kind were ordered. The mere apprehension which the orders for the building of these six vessels, and for the building of about the same number in England, caused to the shipowners of the Northern States made them transfer seven hundred and fifteen of their vessels to British nationality on the spot (letter of Seward to Bigelow, March 15, 1865). As for the French Government, they do not seem to have shared Mr Hall's views of the

extent of their obligations. The Minister of Marine cancelled
M. Arman's authority to arm the vessels on October 22, 1863.
On May 12, 1864, at the sitting of the *Corps Législatif*,
the "orateur" of the Government gave his most positive
assurances that Arman's ships should not go out of French
ports unless it was clearly shown that their destination in no
way affected the principles of neutrality, which the French
Government wished to rigorously observe towards the belligerents.   Only one of these vessels (the *Sphinx*) ever reached
the agents of the South, and this was through the negligence
of the Danish and not of the French Government. The
Government of this country, confronted by the alarm which
the issue of the *Alabama* and the *Florida* from our ports had
created in the merchant navy of the Northern States, and
clearly perceiving that if the term "neutrality" implied anything at all, it implied that war-vessels should not be supplied
by neutral subjects, took the vigorous steps which were mentioned earlier in this essay, and subsequently got an act
passed which expressly forbade ship-*building* for belligerents.
We cannot lose sight of the cardinal fact that the supply of
the *hull* of a war-vessel to the belligerent is the main point.
If we consider the case of a war between England and Russia,
it would be hard to contend that the Hamburg shipbuilders
would not commit a breach of neutrality in supplying Russia
with the hulls of war-vessels, provided the ships were not
(*a*) commissioned or (*β*) equipped during their brief journey
to a Russian port, as Mr Hall contends.

This is a question which the persons most competent to
judge, as we shall now show, have feared will concern this
country most seriously in the future. We close the discussion of this branch of the subject with two quotations from
somewhat interesting sources. The first one emanates from
Sir W. Harcourt in the "Report of the Neutrality Laws
Commissioners, 1868." In contending against the proposals
of the rest of the Commissioners to make the building of

ships for belligerents illegal in the neutral country, he says, "But it will be argued that if the equipping, arming, and despatching of such vessels is to be prohibited, it is necessary, on the principle *obsta principiis*, to extend the prohibition to the earlier stages of the transaction. That reasoning does not carry conviction to my mind ; the arming, equipping, and despatching are conspicuous acts directly and obviously connected with the belligerent intent. *To build is nothing, unless the vessel be armed and despatched ; it is in these acts that the real breach of neutrality consists.* The law should lay its hands on the immediate offence, and not be astute to search out its *remote sources and springs.* To attempt to do so involves consequences which will be politically difficult and dangerous."

The other quotation is from a document which no one can impeach on the score of its possessing an unpractical or merely academic origin. The " memorial " to which we refer was drawn up and signed by no less than thirty-one of the leading shipowners of Liverpool, who felt strongly that their most vital interests would be jeopardized in the next great war that should befall us if the law remained as it was, and whose motives were certainly not those of merely sentimental faddists. The document is headed as follows :—

" Memorial from thirty-one shipowning firms in Liverpool, June 9, 1863, to Earl Russell, Principal Secretary for Foreign Affairs.

" Your memorialists, who are deeply interested in British shipping, view with dismay the probable future consequences of a state of affairs which permits a foreign belligerent to construct in, and send to sea from, British ports vessels of war in contravention of the provisions of the existing law. That the immediate effect of placing at the disposal of that foreign belligerent a *very small number* of steam-cruisers has been to paralyze the mercantile marine of a powerful maritime and naval nation, inflicting within a few months losses, direct and indirect, on its shipowning and mercantile interests which years of peace may prove inadequate to retrieve. That your memorialists cannot shut their eyes to the probability that in any future war between England and a foreign power, however insignificant in naval strength, the example now set by subjects of her Majesty while England is neutral may be followed by citizens of other countries, neutral when England is belligerent ; and that the *attitude of helplessness*, in which her Majesty's Government have declared their inability to detect and punish breaches of the law notoriously committed by certain of her Majesty's subjects, may hereafter be successfully imitated by the Governments of those other countries in answer to English remonstrances."

Supporters of the theory of the "intolerable responsibility of interference" will do well to read this passage.

"That the experience of late events has proved to the conviction of your memorialists that the possession by a belligerent of swift steam-cruisers under no necessity, actual or conventional, to visit the possibly blockaded home ports of that belligerent, but *able to obtain all requisite supplies from neutrals*, will become a weapon of offence against which no preponderance of naval strength can effectually guard, and the severity of which will be felt *in the ratio of the shipping and mercantile wealth* of the nation against whose mercantile marine the efforts of those steam-cruisers may be directed.

"That the effect of a future war with any power thus enabled to purchase, prepare, and refit vessels of war in neutral ports will inevitably be to transfer to neutral flags that portion of the sea-carrying trade of the world which is now enjoyed by your memorialists and by other British shipowners.

"That over and above the chances of pecuniary loss to themselves, your memorialists share in the regret with which a law-regarding community must naturally look on successful attempts to evade the provisions of an Act of Parliament passed for a single and simple purpose, but which has been found not to give the Executive all the powers needed for its effective execution.

"That your memorialists would accordingly respectfully urge upon your lordship the expediency of proposing to Parliament to sanction the introduction of such amendments into the Foreign Enlistment Act as may have the effect of giving greater power to the Executive, to prevent the construction in British ports of ships destined for the use of belligerents. And your memorialists would further suggest to your lordship the importance of endeavouring to secure the assent of the Governments of the United States of America and of *other foreign countries* to the adoption of similar regulations in those countries also."

In reply to this fair-minded, practical, and most prophetic document, Mr Hammond was directed to state "that in Lord Russell's opinion the Foreign Enlistment Act is effectual for all reasonable purposes, and to the full extent to which international law or comity can require." It is possible that some doubts as to the correctness of this opinion may have beclouded the minds of the thirty-one shipowners, when shortly afterwards the Government paid £3,000,000 as compensation for the shortcomings of that same Foreign Enlistment Act.

The "memorial" is particularly instructive from the glaring contrast it presents to the remarks of Sir W. Harcourt on the same subject which have been previously set out, and further from its strong corroboration of the views we have just advocated concerning the importance of the hull. It will be noticed that the shipowners, unaccustomed to the nice distinctions of analytical jurisprudists, bluntly allude to "successful attempts to evade the provisions of an Act of Parliament passed for a single and simple purpose, but which has been found not to give the Executive all the powers needed for its effective execution."

In other words, the Act did not forbid the building of the ship for the belligerent by the neutral, which was the main thing, but only forbade the arming of the ship by him, which was merely an accessory. The Liverpool merchants, who had seen the owners of 715 American merchant-vessels change their nationality merely from the apprehension of three vessels built in England and six in France (five of which were never allowed to depart), seem to have felt instinctively that here there was something wrong, and it may be that other people could be found who would agree with them. Sir W. Harcourt, on the contrary, as we have seen, says, " To build is nothing unless the vessel be armed and despatched ; it is in these acts that the real breach of neutrality consists. The law should lay its hands on the immediate offence, and not be astute to search out its remote sources and springs."

The conclusion we draw from the whole matter is that it is not true that the ground principles of neutrality admit of the sale of war-ships to a belligerent by a neutral subject, provided that they are not commissioned before they leave the neutral port. On the contrary, those principles are flatly opposed to any such trade which in practice reduces neutrality to a hollow mockery. The growing custom against that trade has arisen from a better perception of the real nature of the ground principles of neutrality. If the fears of the Liverpool shipowners were well-founded, it is clear that it would be of enormous advantage to this country to promote a general International convention so that the law on these points might be settled by general agreement as was done by the Treaty of Paris in 1856, concerning other points of neutrality law. It is noteworthy that in 1870 Lord Granville proposed some such convention to Prince Bismarck. If the convention does meet, the following rough outline may perhaps give some idea of the proposals which may come up for discussion.

1. The contracting Powers undertake that they will each provide themselves with municipal laws (in case such laws do not already exist) whereby in the event of any of the said

Powers occupying the position of neutrality, their subjects may be effectively restrained from supplying either belligerent with arms or munitions of war, or materials for the construction of the same, or with horses or their accoutrements. They further undertake that such laws shall be rigorously enforced.

2. The said Powers having regard to the enormous and unique capacity for the destruction of maritime commerce possessed by steam-vessels, hereby undertake that in the event of any of them occupying the position of neutrality they will exercise the most vigorous surveillance to prevent their subjects from building ships for either belligerent which are capable of being used as war-vessels, or from selling such vessels ready-made, to either belligerent, or from arming or equipping or despatching such vessels for either belligerent.

3. The said Powers further engage that if any of them, being in the position of belligerency, shall have established an effective blockade of any of their enemy's ports, the rest of the said Powers which are in the position of neutrality, shall provide themselves with municipal laws whereby if any of their subjects attempt a breach of such blockade, they shall be deemed to have committed a criminal offence, provided that it shall be shown—

(*a*) That the blockade was effective at the date of the alleged offence;

(*b*) That there was proof of *scienter* on the part of the alleged offender.

Further regulations would probably be proposed concerning—

(*a*) The supply of coal to war-vessels in neutral ports.

(*b*) The reception of such vessels and their equipment or armament in neutral ports.

There is no subject which more frequently serves as a butt for the facetious, both in the legal profession and among the laity, than that of International Law. Prince Bismarck, for example, mentions "hunting up some old fogeys who have written on International Law" when in want of an excuse for having caused the sinking of some English vessels in the Franco-German War. The fact that there is among nations no "Austinian Sovereign[1]," with his accompanying "positive laws," his "sanctions," his "power to abolish other sovereigns," and all the other paraphernalia of that juristic Frankenstein, is sufficient to blind the technically minded to the existence of International Law as a hard fact in the life of States. Such persons usually agree with the Swiss delegate at the *Alabama* Arbitration, who thought that International Law was "evolved in each case by an inductive process," *i.e.* was made up as one went on.

It may be noted here, entirely parenthetically, that the total immersion of English constitutional lawyers in the baptismal font of Austinian theories of sovereignty, has been attended with some extremely awkward results in the case of the protectorates established by Great Britain over Zanzibar, Brunei, and the Somali coast. The persons who were responsible in the matter, acting under the influence of the Austinian twaddle as to the "indivisibility of sovereignty," and ignoring the fact that it is a very far cry from the sovereignty of the Queen in council to that of some naked savage seated on a mat of the type of the late Lobengula, or of the Sultan of Brunei, have caused the powers of the Crown to be expressly limited, so as to exclude all jurisdiction over foreigners in those barbarous countries in either civil or criminal matters. The inexpediency of this absence of jurisdiction is manifest, but the reason of it is to be found in the theory that the sovereignty of Great Britain is only "delegated" in such cases, and therefore cannot be exercised over persons who are not subjects of the "delegating power," *i.e.* of the savage

---

[1] A term in English jurisprudence. John Austin is the Grand Lama of English jurisprudence in whom "except a man believe faithfully, he shall perish juristically."

aforesaid.   The French and the Germans suffer from no such Austinian delusions as regards their protectorates.

We would also observe parenthetically, that if the late John Austin, in addition to his other mental gifts, had possessed the faintest spark of humour, he could not, with the early history of the nineteenth century before his eyes, have solemnly dubbed International Law in his system as " Positive International Morality." Considering the canonical position of this personage in English jurisprudence, it is only after considerable hesitation that we have ventured to make the foregoing remarks.

In determining whether it is really incumbent on a neutral government to make the reform we are advocating, it must be borne in mind that the very conception of neutrality has its roots in a barbarous past, only removed from the present time by some two hundred and fifty years, and it has been slowly and painfully evolved from a period when the only restraint on non-neutral acts was the threat of immediate war. Mr Hall quotes a case in support of this fact, as recently as 1677, in which this country, when neutral, not only allowed the impressment of recruits by the French within its territory, but, further, placed Edinburgh Castle at their disposal till the ships were ready to transport the men. This being so, it cannot but be that a code of rules which took its rise amid such circumstances will inevitably bear many a mark of the beast, and it should be the aim of all who desire the progress of humanity to eliminate those marks from the system of International Law (whenever an opportunity occurs for doing so), by appealing, not to outworn precedents, which are often but a wretched compromise between might and right, but to the ideal standard of justice and of unselfishness.

The rights of humanity and of justice are often openly blasphemed by European statesmen and journalists, who do not blush to openly avow their absolute devotion to Mammon and nothing else.

It would be hard to conceive anything more infamous or low-minded than the leading article in the *Daily Telegraph* of Dec. 11th, 1900. It is a comment on the speech of Count von Bülow—of von Bülow who recently informed the world that Germany "did not want to play the part of Providence" in China and cared for nothing but its own interests. Dealing with another speech of Bülow which breathed precisely the same sentiments the *Daily Telegraph* says that "the remarkable and important speech of Count von Bülow *may be recommended to the plain man as a complete and admirable epitome of the whole spirit and practice of international affairs*.......The Imperial Chancellor frames himself with the happiest skill upon the Bismarckian model both in his policy and his phrases.

"The old-fashioned sophistries of feeling are as much out of place in modern diplomatic business as in a mathematical process or a commercial transaction. In this respect the principles of the Iron Chancellor have laid down once for all the fixed basis of the policy of Berlin, and the Germans are unquestionably right in their contention that the hard doctrine of enlightened selfishness is the only possible foundation of a successful management of foreign affairs—one, that is, aiming at the maximum of *profit* with the minimum of risk and *uninfluenced by any other considerations whatever.*"

(The *Daily Telegraph* clearly agrees with von Bülow that God is altogether a mistake in the New Diplomacy and should be improved away out of its methods altogether.)

"Fickle sentiment," continues the ignoble *Daily Telegraph*, "is the shifting sand upon which no prudent statesman should trust his steps, and simple selfishness, as much a matter of course in diplomacy as in trade, the one solid rock upon which practical statesmanship can be safely established....The more candour in these matters the less cant, and the greater satisfaction on both sides.......The diplomacy expounded with masterly skill by Count von Bülow is not only absolutely legitimate and reasonable from the German point of view but *deserves to be adopted as a model by ourselves in all our international dealings.*"

Let all those persons who believe with the writer that it is a hideous libel on the English people to represent them as such a low-minded and sordid crew thank Heaven that the much-despised " Nonconformist conscience " is a hard fact in England. We also recommend to their notice the words of Cromwell and Carlyle on the conduct of the Dutch in letting out their ships for hire to assist the enemies of their own religion. " God will find them out, they shall not prosper in it. They cannot, unless God and His truth be a mere hearsay of the market."

The German soldiery in China have not been slow to catch the spirit of their betters who directed them "not to play the part of Providence" and to "give no quarter." The *New York Herald* of Feb. 19th, 1901, shows that they have bettered their instructions. That journal's special correspondent says: " It is to the Germans that we must award the laurels of outrage in the campaign.......There was something particularly cold-blooded about their proceedings. They arrived, when the country ought to have been settling down, to avenge the murder of their Minister and to carry out the mandate of the Kaiser. After marching into Peking, leaving their path stained with the blood of hundreds of innocent people who had just ventured to return to their homes, the Germans established a military reign of terror.

" In their section of the city every day there were executions. One day 68 people were shot. They did not hesitate to resort to Oriental methods for the purpose of extracting evidence from witnesses. The treatment of their prisoners, as I can personally testify from what I saw, was most brutal.

" The result of the manner in which the Germans ruled their quarter of the town is apparent, even up to the present time, by its being practically deserted by its inhabitants. As

late as the week I left Peking the Germans had 83 executions
in their quarter. This was rather below than above their
usual average.

"Even the intense cold of the extremely severe winter has
not been able to drive the inhabitants of that section back to
the shelter of their homes. No one can tell how thousands
of these unfortunate outcasts have got through the last few
months in the bleak, inhospitable country which surrounds
Peking."

"The German fatherland," remarked the Kaiser on
April 27th, "is so rich in ideals."

INTERVENTION AMONG STATES.

THE question of the right of interference by one or more States in the affairs of another State may safely be dubbed at the present time as the most nebulous topic in the somewhat nebulous science of International Law. The extreme uncertainty in which the principles of the subject are at present enshrouded has discouraged the fluency even of foreign professors of International Law, and the literary output of these gentlemen on intervention is most scanty in view of the fact that the one especially salient feature in the international history of Europe in this century has been intervention. The part which this country has played in that history has been considerable, and, in the main, most beneficial, although the principles by which our Governments have been guided may be sought in vain in official utterances and despatches. The ministers who have been responsible in the matter have usually contented themselves with repeating in substance the words of the late Lord Palmerston, viz. :—
" The usual rule is non-intervention, but I am not prepared to say that there may not be occasions on which intervention is justifiable." Their principles must be sought for in their international acts.

In order to discuss the subject with even the possibility of arriving at any tangible and profitable result, we submit that three stages are necessary, viz. : (1) A consideration of the analogy which undoubtedly exists between the phenomena

of the international life of modern States, and the phenomena
of the lives of individuals in a modern civilized State. (2) A
consideration of the principal modern instances of intervention
as illustrating that analogy. (3) A deduction of the principles
of intervention based upon that analogy.

The consideration of the first part of the subject necessarily involves some observations of a very elementary
description ;—(1) In every civilized State there is a certain
number of persons of mature age and discretion who can
pay their way and are mentally and physically capable of
managing their own affairs. (*b*) On the other hand, there
are large classes of persons in every State who are under
what is termed a legal disability. These classes include
women (in certain respects), children under age, lunatics
and imbecile persons, convicts, bankrupts, etc. The normal
and natural subjects of disabilities are women and children.
The abnormal subjects are lunatics and imbeciles, convicts
and bankrupts. In both cases the Central Authority of the
State intervenes in the private doings of these persons for
their own or for the general good, and, to a varying degree,
controls their liberty of action. The interference with the
actions of women and children is mainly paternal in character,
and is designed in the interests of the objects of it. The
interference with the other classes is, on the other hand,
mainly defensive or punitive, or both. It is "not for their
own but for their country's good." The next point on which
we would dwell is that, in all these defensive or punitive cases
of disability, there is a point where the State is bound to step
in for its own good. "No man liveth to himself." A man's
house is his castle only up to a certain point, and his right to
preserve his privacy vanishes absolutely before the general
right of humanity. Let us consider the case of colliers living
in adjoining cottages. When one of them cruelly maltreats
his wife, the State intervenes and restricts his liberty for a
couple of years or more. If the collier keeps his children at

home, the State interferes and compels him to send them to school. If a man makes of his house a gambling den, or a brothel, his right to the privacy of his "castle" is rudely interfered with by the civil authorities. Liberty exists only within the law among citizens, and there is a point where that liberty vanishes because it runs counter to the general good. Now, our main position in this essay is that the international life of States is nothing more than the life of individuals "writ large." If we follow out this idea we shall find ourselves in conflict at once with what we regard as the crowning fiction of International Law, viz. :—that there are no degrees in independence in the eye of International Law, and that all independent States according to that law have a perfect equality of status. According to this theory there is no difference between the status of Turkey and that of Russia. Now, although epigrams of this kind are doubtless most soothing to the national pride—*e.g.*, of members of the Swiss Republic—it is impossible to shut our eyes to the fact that in practice they are nothing more than fictions which are absolutely disregarded when a need arises for settling international matters. It is as absurd to assert this fiction as it would be to assert that in the modern State all its members are in an identical state of independence. Are there no wards or minors or lunatics or imbeciles or convicts whose independence of action must of necessity be interfered with? Let us now cast our eyes over some of the main facts of the history, during the last century alone, of France and Spain and Portugal and Italy and Belgium and Switzerland and Holland, and above all, of Turkey. We submit that here there are instances in abundance of States which have been dangerous lunatics or incapable imbeciles or hopeless bankrupts or helpless minors or culpable criminals. There has been, it is true, no officially established machinery as in the modern civilized State for the punishment of criminals, the guardianship of minors or the restraining of lunatics, yet the welfare of other States has imperiously demanded that this work should be somehow carried out. It was this necessity which produced seventy-five per cent. of what we call the " Interventions " of the nineteenth century. The same fiction whereby all States are deemed equally independent connotes the assertion that they are all of sound mind and competent to manage their affairs in a rational manner. There is no fact more certain in modern history than the lunacy or imbecility under which some States have laboured and continue to labour. It will suffice to mention such instances as—

(1) Poland. The lunatic perseverance with which Poland clung to what was called the *liberum veto*, which hopelessly paralysed the machinery of legislation, may be realized when we come to consider the fact that no measure could be passed by their Parliament as long as there were any dissentients at all. Consequently when it became absolutely necessary to pass some measure the procedure, according to Mr Carlyle, for overcoming the scruples of obstinate opposers consisted in running the latter through the body. Now, if affairs were really managed in Poland after this fashion, it is difficult to feel any more surprise at the partition of Poland than at the compulsory detention of an undoubted lunatic.

(2) France. There is a wide distinction to be drawn between occasional domestic cataclysms in a State and permanent derangement. Thus there is a great difference between the character of the intervention of other European Powers in her affairs in 1792 and that of 1815.

In the first case the bulk of the people were endeavouring to rid themselves of a political system which was in many respects of an incredibly barbarous and tyrannical description. If the people in the course of that struggle showed themselves bereft of a sense of pity, it should be always remembered that the acts of their rulers for centuries (with their private gibbets in each village) had killed any such feelings they might have possessed. Although the State was passing through a fearful internal crisis it was still able to discharge its external duties, and the intervention of the despotic powers in 1792 was one of political despotism against political freedom.

This interference with France on the part of Austria and Prussia in her dark hour of struggle for political liberty should be borne in mind by those who are too ready to condemn the somewhat bandit-like behaviour she afterwards displayed to those countries. If France at that time, as we firmly believe, really represented the eternal rebellion of the free-minded citizen against the stifling weight of a hereditary noblesse which battened on the labour and the money of the people, while it denied them any share in the government and denied them common justice, it is no matter for surprise to us that in a little while the people who were illumined, if only for a time, by such splendid ideas of political liberty, should have not only beaten off their "legitimate" assailants, but should have crushed their outworn political systems like eggshells in the Napoleonic wars which shortly ensued. The ideas of the triumphant Puritans of the English Revolution on religious toleration, on the iniquity of preferring caste to merit, and on even-handed justice for all were fundamentally the same as the main ideas of the French Revolutionists, and in each case the same magical success attended them.

In 1815 the intervention of the Allies was quite another matter. Napoleon had gazed to some purpose on the real political disabilities of many of the States of Europe. He had tested the "Sovereign independence" of Spain, and its crazy structure of government had fallen at the first touch. His empire over other sovereign States, and his creation of fresh States, were all alike the result of the political incompetence of the countries in which he intervened. They were all supposed in theory to be sovereign and independent and equal. In fact they nearly all belonged to some of the classes under disability which we have enumerated above.

The French under Napoleon were not a success from an economic standpoint as the guardians of the continent. Many of their ablest administrators and generals were mere "voleurs" (as Napoleon himself admitted) who cared only for plunder, and their chief allowed his passions to lead him to the impossible policy of the Berlin decrees. Even the best friends of the French nation would admit, we believe, the absurdity of supposing that this luxurious, dapper, and pleasure-loving nation could have inherited the administrative mantle of the Roman proconsuls.

After the "chute" of Napoleon France was treated by the Board of States, which overcame her, as a kind of unjust guardian who was obliged to make *restitutio in integrum*.

(3) Turkey. This country is the principal instance on which we rely as justifying our dissent from the views of the many writers who hold that intervention in the cause of humanity in the internal affairs of a sovereign State is never permissible.

The most lucid exponent of the views of this body of writers is probably Mr W. E. Hall. "International Law," he says, "professes to be concerned only with the relations of States to each other. Tyrannical conduct of a Government towards its subjects, massacres and brutality in a civil war, or religious persecution are acts which have nothing to do directly or indirectly with such relations." We submit at the outset that this is not true. No State lives to itself. If we try this assertion by the civil test it immediately falls to the ground. If a man ill-treats his children within the sacred precincts of his house or beats his wife with the poker, no one will assert that conduct of this kind is no concern of his neighbours. We do not suggest that in international affairs all tyrannical conduct or all massacres justify intervention. In civil life mere domestic squabbles or incompatibility of temper does not justify interference by the State. As we have previously remarked, there is a great difference between a temporary political upheaval and a settled system of barbarous misrule.

Mr Hall then continues, "On what ground can International Law take cognizance of them? Apparently on one only, if indeed it be competent to take cognizance of them at all. It may be supposed to declare that acts of the kind mentioned are so inconsistent with the character of a moral being as to constitute a public scandal which the body of States, or one or more States as representative of it, are competent to suppress.

" The supposition strains the fiction that States which are under International Law form a kind of society to an extreme point. Not only in fact is the propriety or impropriety of an intervention directed against an alleged scandal judged by the popular mind upon considerations of sentiment to the exclusion of law, but sentiment has been allowed to influence the more deliberately formed opinion of jurists. That the latter should have taken place cannot be too much regretted. In giving their sanction to interventions of the kind in question, jurists have imported an aspect of legality to a species of intervention which makes a deep inroad into one of the cardinal doctrines of International Law. It is unfortunate that publicists have not laid down broadly and unanimously that no intervention is legal except for the purpose of self-preservation unless a breach of the law as between States has taken place, or unless the whole body of civilized States have concurred in authorising it." (*International Law*, p. 303.)

This somewhat lengthy extract is another good instance of Mr Hall's utilitarian views of the basis of International Law which we have previously noted in another essay.

Professor Walker also says (*Science of International Law*, p. 151), " The rule regularly progresses towards more general recognition that non-intervention in the internal affairs of a State is a law which admits of *no exception to* foreign Powers, so long as the operations of that State are confined in their effect to the limits of the national territory." As an instance of the opposite view on this subject, we now give an extract from Professor Arntz :—

"When a Government, although acting within its rights of sovereignty, violates the rights of humanity, either by measures contrary to the interests of other States, or by an excess of cruelty and injustice, which is a blot on our civilization, the right of intervention may lawfully be exercised, for, however worthy of respect are the rights of State Sovereignty and Independence, there is something yet more worthy of respect, and that is the right of humanity or of human society, which must not be outraged."

In judging between these two views, it may perhaps be well to recall the events of three or four years ago in Armenia. One of the most ordinary incidents of that blood-stained and disgraceful period was correctly depicted by a French cartoon of the German Emperor, after his friendly visit to the Sultan, entitled, "A day's sport with his friend, Abdul, in Armenia." On the ground, before the two monarchs, were laid the results of a sort of battue of Armenian Christian women and children which had just taken place. There were many such battues about that time, yet, according to Mr Hall, because collective action of the Great Powers was prevented by national jealousies, and by the friendly attitude, *e.g.*, of the Emperor William to the Sultan, it was no business of any of the individual States to interpose and put an end to murderous horrors, worthy of the Maoris of New Zealand, and compared to which, in the number of its victims, the Spanish Inquisition was as nothing.

It is noteworthy that the German sovereign on the occasion we have mentioned proceeded forthwith to visit Jerusalem and to inform the world in a fit of religious fervour produced by his surroundings that the German Empire was "bathed in the light of the cross," and that

" he and his house would serve the Lord." We may here remark by the way that the latest winter madness with which a large section of the English Press has recently been seized shows itself in fulsome and extravagant adulation of this person. The *Morning Post* was especially to the fore with weak-minded and pusillanimous flattery. If our Press continues in this strain the continent will begin to believe that the nation is as obsequious as the leader-writer of the *Morning Post*. Let us recall the fact which the French *Figaro* brought out with great clearness on Feb. 15th, 1901. "It is but yesterday that the Emperor in urging the increase of his navy said that England was the trade rival and the political adversary of Germany." We fear the Danai even when they bring Black Eagles.

It will be noticed that Mr Hall speaks with contempt of the " considerations of sentiment, to the exclusion of law," which operate on the public mind. We are fain to confess that if the principles of International Law teach us to remain passive spectators of Armenian atrocities for the sake of a legal fiction, we prefer the rule of sentiment to the rule of law.

The intervention of the Powers, in 1827, to put an end to Turkish misrule in Greece, although nominally based upon the inconvenience and damage to trade which the insurrection was causing, was produced in the main by the immortal ode of Byron on Greece and by his tragic death. It was a collective act of humanity on the part of the three Powers.

Greece was continually maltreated by its self-constituted guardian, and the people of England refused to remain passively contemplating the torture of a people, to whose ancestors Europe owes so vast a debt, by a horde of half-savage Mussulmans. Mr C. A. Fyffe, in his *History of Modern Europe*, thus describes the state of things in Greece at that time: "The evils to which the Greek population was exposed whenever Greeks and Turks lived together were those which brutalized or degraded the Christian races in every Ottoman province. There was no redress for injury inflicted by a Mohammedan official or neighbour. If a wealthy Turk murdered a Greek in the fields, burnt down his house and outraged his family, there was no Court where the offender could be brought to justice. A Mohammedan landowner might terrorize the entire population around him, carry off the women, flog and imprison the men, and yet feel that he had committed no offence against the law, for no law existed but the Koran, no Turkish Court of Justice but that of the Kadi, where the complaint of the Christian passed unheeded.

"This was the monstrous relation that existed between the dominant and the subject nationalities, not in Greece only, but in every part of the Ottoman Empire where Mohammedans and Christians inhabited the same districts."

Surely it is absurd to assert, with facts of this kind before our eyes, that as long as the cruelties which the Turks practise on their subject peoples are confined only to those peoples, International Law is bound to erect a sort of "Wall of China" around the Ottoman Empire, and to forbid another State to interfere to prevent such hideous crimes, unless it can induce all the other Great Powers to act with it.

What is the basis for all this reverence for the inviolability of a State?

A French writer has well said :—" The State is a thing contingent, relative, eminently variable both in its limits and in its internal form. A State perhaps is simply the product of violence and has no other merit except its existence."

We entirely fail to see why a State such as Turkey, which, as regards many of its dominions, is merely "the product of violence," should command that religious respect for its personality which inspires such writers as M. Carnazza Amari. We might say with Talleyrand, if it were urged that such a

State "must exist," "We do not see the necessity." Guizot writes as follows on the state of things in Turkey. "In order that Governments and peoples may act effectually on each other by counsels, examples, meetings and diplomatic engagements, there must be between them a certain degree of analogy and sympathy in their customs, ideas and sentiments and in the great features and the great currents of civilization and social life. There is no resemblance between European Christians and Turks. They can, from necessity, from political reasons, live in peace side by side. They always remain strangers to each other. Though they have ceased fighting they have not begun to comprehend each other. The Turks have been nothing in Europe but destructive and barren conquerors incapable of making the populations who have fallen under their yoke like themselves and equally incapable of letting themselves assimilate to them or to their neighbours.

"How long shall this spectacle last of this radical incompatibility which ruins and depopulates such fine countries and condemns so many millions of men to such miseries?"

It is somewhat curious to pass from the perusal of facts of this kind into the atmosphere of legal fictions which writers such as Carnazza Amari have endeavoured to create around the subject of intervention. According to him, "A nation which attempts to interfere with another encounters the national sovereignty of the other which alone has the right to judge the acts of its subjects, so that the foreign State in order to exercise its intervention must destroy this sovereignty to usurp its powers."

Elsewhere he says:—"Their power halting at their own frontiers, it is never permissible for them to extend it over the territory of another."

And again:—"Every nation is wholly free within its own territory without any other jurisdiction or sovereignty over it than those of the nation. *Barbarous or civilized, lenient or violent, reactionary or progressive, it is she, and she alone, who has the right to govern the State."*

M. Amari overlooks the fact that "she" is, after all, only a portion of humanity, and that her independence is a thing which may be forfeited or interfered with if she endeavours from imbecility or malice to run counter to the common laws of humanity in her behaviour to her subjects, or to foreigners within her gates.   M. Amari continues :—" Every corrective action of a foreign State constitutes a violent intrusion in the domain of another ; a supreme tyranny of the strong over the weak, the usurpation and the seizure of sovereign powers to which the intruder has no right, the exercise of an unlawful power, a servitude imposed by the oppressor on the oppressed."

It is natural that the views of M. Amari on the subject of intervention should be somewhat strongly pronounced owing to the infamous system of intervention in the affairs of his own country on the part of Austria up to quite a recent date, but after we have made all allowances for this fact we still submit that in some cases of intervention it would be just as reasonable to talk in this way about oppressor and oppressed as it would be for some Bermondsey drunkard to harangue the police about their oppression of him when he is arrested for the grievous bodily injury he has caused to his wife.   The criminal work of International Law has to be done sooner or later by some one.

The same writer then proceeds to give utterance to the " Chinese Wall" theory of State life.   "Whatever happens inside the walls," he says in effect, " is nothing to do with you."   He also reproduces the fiction that the State has a kind of separate personality which is quite distinct from that of its component members.   " The individuality of its members is absorbed in that of the nation to which they belong, and which represents them in their totality and in the manifestations of the activity which takes effect outside the State to the detriment of another nation. This is the reason why States can only enforce the law as regards other States in the sphere of their *international* activity; that is to say, they can repel all acts of another State which are to their own disadvantage, but beyond that they have no jurisdiction and no power.

"From this it results that the internal autonomy which arises in the relation of governor and governed or of party and party within the body politic of the nation is not subject to the jurisdiction of stranger States because the stranger has no jurisdiction.

"Intervention signifies the substitution of the stranger State for the internal autonomy of the nation, and that the former should be allowed to arraign the internal conduct of another State should never be allowed in the law of nations either as a rule or as an exception."

All this is entirely opposed to the truth that lies in the saying that "no State lives to itself." Nations are always passing judgments on the "interior conduct" of other nations, and it is mere twaddle to talk about "lack of jurisdiction" over the offending State if the spirit of humanity is roused by its atrocious behaviour.

The right to liberty and independence exists only within the law alike in civil and in international life.

The present intervention of the Powers in China may fitly be cited as an illustration. If we are to be guided by the multitude of writers who decry intervention in the cause of humanity under any circumstances, we must regard the slaughter of missionaries and the attempted massacre of the inmates of embassies as purely domestic matters which do not concern outsiders, and in regard to which, outsiders (as M. Amari puts it) have no jurisdiction whatever.

China is not *de facto* an independent State, nor is it of sound political mind. On the contrary its political system is in a crazed condition of senile decay, and consequently the intervention of the European Powers to save the lives of their own subjects, and to ultimately abolish the barbarous Chinese polity, is undoubtedly in the interests of humanity, although the majority of the intervening Powers may be guided mainly by motives of self-interest. It is absurd to talk about lack of jurisdiction in the face of impending massacres of embassies.

The question of the loss by a State of its right to freedom from interference through criminal conduct is closely allied to the question of a similar loss which is unfortunately entailed on a State through weakness or imbecility. One of the commonest international incidents of the nineteenth century has been the occasional settlement of the affairs of some of these States by a sort of " Board " of their superiors.

We now proceed to briefly touch on the principal cases of intervention in Europe in the last century, as recorded in detail by that humane and sagacious American, Chancellor Kent, whose volume is a veritable oasis among works on International Law.

The wholesale remodelling of European territorial arrangements by Napoleon is the first instance we shall quote. Among his " wards " were Spain and Portugal, the Republics of Italy, the Kingdom of Westphalia, the Duchy of Warsaw, the League of the Rhine, the Kingdoms of Naples, Holland, Belgium, etc., etc. When his power collapsed a large part of it was " taken over " by the Allies. They were responsible for the junction of Norway to Sweden, of Genoa to Sardinia, of Venice to Austria, of Belgium to Holland, of Poland to Russia, and for the partial dismemberment of Saxony. The principal objection to their method of thus settling the affairs of these minor States of Europe lay in the fact that the territories thus divided were mapped out with no regard whatever to the national instincts of their inhabitants. The inability of many of the countries, whose affairs were then temporarily settled, to successfully manage their own affairs has since been demonstrated. We do not propose to touch more than incidentally here on the terribly threadbare topics of the Holy Alliance and of the Congresses of Laybach, Troppau and Verona from 1818–20, at which the infamous resolutions were taken against the wishes of this country to interfere in the cause of despotic government in Spain, Portugal, and Italy. It is one thing to interfere to stop the constantly repeated butchery of women and children by half-civilized religious fanatics as in the case of Armenia, but it is quite another thing to interfere, as did the Holy Alliance in a grandmotherly fashion with Spain and Naples, because the intervening Powers disliked the progress of ideas from autocracy to popular government. The principal instances of this class of intervention in the last century are the intervention of Austria in Naples 1820, that of France in Spain 1822, that of Austria in Italy 1831–2, and again in 1849, and that of Russia in Hungary 1849. The last case is more noteworthy and on a larger scale than any of the others. The Magyars, who are a strong, capable, and independent race of different origin to the Austrians, made so determined a bid for independence that they would undoubtedly have overcome the resistance of the parent State, or, rather of the sovereign State, but for the forcible interference of Russia in the interests of autocracy. On this occasion the friends of liberty in England, who wished to assist the Hungarians, were informed by Lord Palmerston that "so far as the courtesies of international intercourse may permit us it is our duty, especially when an opinion is asked, to state our opinions founded on the experience of this country. We are not entitled to interpose in any manner that will commit this country to embark on these hostilities." The same statesman, it is true, had previously justified the intervention of England and France in the affairs of the Peninsula in 1834 by asserting that in any quarrel every State had a "right" in International Law to take sides with one party. England stood aloof and the Hungarians were robbed by the force of Russian arms of the fruits of their brave struggles for liberty, but the time may yet come when we may deplore the absence of a strong independent State instead of a bankrupt, senile and priest-ridden one in that part of Europe as a bulwark against Russian aggression.

As regards the delights of the Austrian yoke to which the Czar re-consigned the Magyars, no better illustration of them can be found than the case of the Austrian occupation of Italy. Italian women were publicly flogged in the streets, the peasantry were maltreated in every way, and when the opportunity came, the inhabitants showed their deadly hatred of the Austrians and their system of rule.   In face of what we have written about the subject of Russia and Hungarian independence it is no doubt open to the foreign critic to point to the present Boer War as a flagrant instance of the same sort on the part of Great Britain.

We submit, however, that if the facts of the case are closely considered it will be seen that the Boers were in a position which resembled that of the French noblesse before the Revolution in some very essential matters.   In each case we see a privileged hereditary minority treating an unprivileged majority as a sort of milch cow (in the words of Mr Balfour). The minority fattens itself and grows rich on the produce of the labours of the majority and consistently refuses the latter either equal justice or equal political privileges in order to maintain its enviable position in the State.

Under these circumstances there has been much talk of "European intervention" in the Transvaal War.   Never has there been a more ridiculous proposal or a greater display of false sentiment.   The Boer republics owed the powers of self-government that had been bestowed upon them to the free grace of a great Empire.   They proceeded to make use of those powers to treat the citizens of that Empire, as far as possible, as the feudal lords of the middle ages treated their

serfs, or as the Israelites (whom they were always endeavouring to copy) treated the Gibeonites. When the Empire
objected to this and proceeded to enforce a remedy, nothing
less than a hysterical shriek for intervention was raised by
continental journalists who likened the struggle to the
American War of Independence. If we regard the unfranchised
Uitlander population who paid the taxes and had no votes as
filling the position of the Americans in that war, the parallel
might possibly be justified, but not otherwise. If the intervention had taken place, it would have been mainly to enable
the Boers to "wallop their own niggers," which is not a very
elevated object for a great international movement.

The three interventions of Great Britain in Portugal are
good instances of a justifiable settlement of the affairs of a
weak minor State by a powerful one. In 1826 the country,
being more or less in the infancy of its newly-acquired
political liberty, found its executive powers unable to resist
the plotting of the friends of autocracy, and the Government
asked for the assistance of England. The country had passed
through long years of anarchy, and England intervened to
give a helping hand to law and order. Again, in 1834, when
France and England jointly interfered in Spain and Portugal,
the Governments were in a state of helplessness. Don Carlos,
the Spanish Pretender, had entered Portugal to raise an army
for his designs on the Spanish throne. The Portuguese
Government confessed their disapproval of this, and their
inability to stop it, and offered to allow a Spanish force to
enter the country to effect this purpose. In an abnormal
case of this kind—which was not a violent political upheaval,
bringing peace and a new order of things in its train, but was
merely a desultory squabble with nothing to be hoped for but
years of guerilla warfare and general chaos—it is at least
arguable that England and France were justified in stepping
in to patch up the decaying fabric, and to help to rivet the
ricketty timbers of government together.

P.   6

The English intervention of 1847, in Portugal, was as justifiable as the other two which preceded it. It was thus explained by the English Government: " The object of our interference was a recall of the Parliament in which the people could state their grievances, and restore the battles of political party to the legitimate arena of the Senate. In consequence of these views, the intervention was not confined to the forcible termination of the rebellion. The London Conference insisted on the formation of a new ministry prepared to concede liberal measures of reform to the country."

The English intervention in Belgium, in 1831, is the next topic which we shall discuss. When the union of Belgium and Holland turned out, for racial reasons, to be an unhappy failure, the European Powers, with the exception of France and England, appear to have been in favour of the maxim, " Those whom the Congress of Vienna hath joined together, let no man put asunder." Earl Grey, on the contrary, in justifying the action of this country, said : " Is a union of the two countries to be kept up where the dispositions of both are so uncongenial, and which was originally founded on a vicious principle ? " (*i.e.*, the principle of treating blood relationship as a secondary matter to geographical position).

" Could the strife for separation be allowed to continue and hazard the peace of Europe ? I hold the principle of non-interference as strongly as I have ever done, but I am not prepared to say there may not be proper exceptions to the rule."

The knot which had been artificially tied by the representatives of the Allies in 1815 was untied by artificial means by England and France in 1831, and in view of the racial antipathies of the ill-assorted couple we do not think that many persons at the present day would affirm that the separation was anything but a beneficial act.

The intervention of Great Britain in Turkish affairs in

1840 and again in 1854 may perhaps be characterized as the only two cases in which this country has, in its continental interventions since 1815, been guided in the main by interested motives which concerned *itself* more than that of the country in whose affairs it has intervened.   In 1840 the circumstances of the intervention were *primâ facie* of an extraordinary character.   The rebellious Pasha of Egypt, Mehemet Ali, had, like the Greeks, been engaged in a long struggle with the Porte, but unlike the Greeks, he was on the point of establishing his independence without any kind of external aid.   On the other hand, no particular benefit to the Egyptians or to anyone else was likely to ensue from this independence.   The rule of the Pasha was ultimately as barbarous as that of the Turks.   There was no particular reason for sympathising with Mehemet in his efforts to substitute the sovereignty of one Oriental despot for another in Egypt.   Moreover, the Powers who were represented at the London Conference had an excellent reason for preserving the Sultan's dominions intact in a well-grounded fear of the dreams of Empire which the Russians were known to possess.   We have no intention of setting out here all the peculiarly cogent reasons which cause the British to regard the possible predominance of Russian influence at Constantinople with the utmost aversion. It will suffice to quote one of the many luminous sentences of Napoleon in his last years on this subject.   " Once mistress of Constantinople Russia gets all the commerce of the Mediterranean, becomes a great naval power, and, God knows what may happen.   Above all the other Powers, Russia is the most to be feared by the English."

The intervention of England in Turkish affairs in 1854 was inspired by the same motives as was that of 1840.   It may be pointed out that in both cases the Government of the Porte has been in the position of an incapable lunatic, unable to manage its own affairs.   The Sultan Mahmud at the time of his death in 1839 was in a state of frenzy over the victories

of Mehemet, and was ready to make shipwreck of his kingdom
in the effort to overthrow him. His successor was most
willing to take the assistance which was offered him by the
four Powers. In 1854 the Porte was so far from being
de facto a sovereign and independent State (whatever it may
have been in theory), that if the two Western Powers had not
taken over the task of intervening in its foreign relations,
its separate existence as a State would have vanished
altogether.

In 1866 Turkish misrule in the Island of Crete produced
a sanguinary disturbance between the inhabitants and their
oppressors. On that occasion the part played by our Government in the cause of humanity was of a somewhat edifying
description. Our ministers had not studied the writings
of international jurists on the theoretical independence and
equality of all States for nothing, and they acted accordingly
on the great fiction "Toute nation est souveraine sur son
propre territoire et il n'y a aucune juridiction au-dessus d'elle."
According to Calvo, " The concert of Europe fell through in
great part owing to the influence of England which protested
its desire to observe a strict neutrality in the quarrel, and not
to give any assistance to one or the other side, and which
went so far as to refuse to allow women and children exposed
to be massacred by the Turks to embark on their ships of
war" (309). The freedom from jurisdiction of a State is like
that of a householder, viz., conditional on the observation of
due humanity to his members.

From 1875–77 the state of affairs in the countries which
are now known as Servia, Bulgaria, Roumania, Montenegro,
Bosnia, the Herzegovina, and Eastern Roumelia, occupied the
attention of the European Powers. When a joint intervention
on the part of Germany, Austria-Hungary, Russia, France,
Italy, and England was proposed, Lord Derby instructed
Sir H. Elliott, at Constantinople, that "a mediation of this
kind is not at all compatible with the independent authority

of the Porte in its own territory. This proceeding furnishes in short a motive for insurrection as a means of exciting foreign sympathy against Turkish rule, and it is not improbable that this intervention may pave the way for ulterior intermeddling in the interior affairs of the Empire. But as the Porte has prayed your excellency not to hold aloof from the affair, the Government of Her Majesty sees that it has no other alternative." M. Calvo has well said that as a result of that conference :—

"Donc l'Europe réunie en tribunal à Berlin en 1878 a solennellement reconnu le principe de l'intervention collective entr'un état et ses sujets dans l'intérêt de l'humanité et surtout dans celui des nationalités."

The relations of the Powers at the Berlin Conference to the Petty States which they then called into existence are those of guardian and ward. "If uncontrolled by Europe, the animosities and jealousies of Greeks, Bulgars, Serbs, and Macedonians, preventing them from acting in concert and leading to internecine conflicts, might quickly lead to the reimposition of the Turkish yoke upon her former provinces or more probably to an international conflict for the partition of Turkey, disturbing the peace of the world and fatal to the independence of these little States." The same sort of guardianship has been asserted by the United States over the smaller States of Central and Southern America in the Monroe Doctrine. The Monroe Doctrine is nothing more than an expansion of the natural sense of guardianship felt by the United States as the predominant power in that part of the world for the minor States whose institutions are more or less modelled on their own, which is aroused when a likelihood arises of interference with their liberty or institutions on the part of a foreign Power. Monroe said :—"It is impossible for European Powers to interfere in the affairs of these States, especially on subjects which are for them vital principles, without this affecting the United States."

The United States very nearly came into collision with France when Napoleon III. made the ridiculous attempt to set up an "Emperor of Mexico" in 1861. Mr Seward then said :—"The people of the United States have the firm conviction that progress in this part of the world is not possible except by means of political institutions identical in all the States of the American Continent."

In order to get some idea of the number of European countries whose territorial limits and affairs have been compulsorily settled for them under the guardianship of other Powers in the last century, it will only be necessary to mention Belgium, Holland, Switzerland, France, Luxembourg, Spain, Portugal, Sicily, Naples, Lombardy, Venice, Saxony, Poland, Cracow, Norway and Sweden, Denmark, the Danubian Principalities, the Rhenish States, Turkey, Bosnia, Servia, Roumania, Montenegro, Eastern Roumelia, the Herzegovina, and Greece.

There have been five great meetings of "Boards of Guardians" for this purpose in the course of the century, viz., in 1815, 1831, 1840, 1856, and 1878. Of these by far the most important was that of 1815. Napoleon had brought about what was practically a "re-shuffle" of the cards of the States of Europe, and consequently it remained for the Allies to execute "a fresh deal." The Boards of 1840, 1856, and 1878 have been mainly occupied with the wide subject of the tributary possessions of the Porte. We have already mentioned the Conference of 1831. The principal object of anxiety to the successive Boards has been the preservation of the "balance of power" in Europe. The theory of the "balance of power" is, as everyone knows, of great antiquity, having served as a great political principle of action to the States of Ancient Greece. The object of preserving the balance is to prevent the realization of those "golden dreams of empire" which are always pervading the slumbers of powerful nations. In the middle ages the Thirty Years' War was mainly fought in the cause of the balance of power which was formally recognized as a great principle of International Politics at Westphalia in 1648. Again in 1713 at Utrecht the principle was formally recognized, and it has twice in the nineteenth century been enunciated by Great Britain in Treaties. The theory plainly arises from the strong sense of separate nationality among States. If we cast our eyes once more on the life of individuals in a State, it would seem that the family is the type in civil life of what nation is in the company of States. In the present condition of the human race it can hardly be denied (except by a Tolstoi) that the existence of the sentiment of nationality in the one case and of the sentiment of unity and privacy in the other are two most beneficent factors in public and private life. Great empires over various nationalities such as Louis XIV. imagined and Napoleon realized for a brief period are mainly founded on the essential weakness of the various nations which become absorbed in them. Our own Indian Empire and the Russian Empire are most striking instances of this.

Consequently where a group of nations are more or less on an equality of civilization and their national energies are in a healthy condition, as is the case in Europe, it is natural that they should each view the idea of vassalage to any one predominating member of their body with a dread as great as is the affection they feel for their nationality. It would be hard to argue that the Western States were not justified in 1854 when they interfered to prevent Russia obtaining a power in Europe which would be a constant menace to the independence of the rest of the body of States.

The crushing of a nationality or its forcible absorption by another Power is an act which always produces so universal a shudder among the nations that it would seem to be instinctively revolting to the sense of mankind. Consequently we should incline to affirm that an intervention to preserve the balance of power is a natural and lawful act if its object is to preserve the independence of States against a common danger, or to save one of the number from oppression or extinction. The Austrian tamperings with Italian affairs in 1821, 1831, 1849, and 1859, and the Russian intervention of 1849 in the Hungarian contest belong to this latter category, and the action of the French Emperor in fighting the battle of Custozza for Italian liberties appears to us to have been one of the most meritorious actions in the life of that personage. The opinion of Great Britain on the intervention by Austria of the kind we have indicated may best be understood by the remarks of its Government when the French were illegally dallying in Rome with a body of their troops. "The foreign occupation on which the Court of Rome relies cannot be indefinitely prolonged, nor can an auxiliary force suppress the discontent of a whole population, and even if such means were likely to succeed it is not the kind of pacification which the British Government intends to help to bring about."

The various measures of coercion which Great Britain, in company with the other Great Powers, has been obliged to adopt from time to time in the case of Greece, have usually been for the purpose (as in the case of the "pacific blockade" in 1886) of saving that irresponsible minor State from the effects of its own rashness against the Turk.

The root of all the evils that have befallen Greece since the intervention of the Allies in 1827 lies in the action of the Duke of Wellington. The Iron Duke, whose *wooden look* has been so well described by Byron, cared nothing for the "splendours of old Greece" and had no belief in the power of the feelings of nationality. Through fear of Russian influence in the new State he drew its boundaries with so niggardly a hand that it has been almost impossible for the new State to support itself and pay its way. This is the cause of the frequent Grecian eruptions which disturb Europe.

We have already briefly touched on the decayed and occasionally chaotic state of the Kingdom of Spain and Portugal. As regards the incapacity of the Spanish Government to prevent insurrections from smouldering on in a futile and desultory manner with no result but general disorder it is noteworthy, in view of the latest case of intervention (viz. that of the United States in Cuba), that President Grant, as far back as 1874, said, "the deplorable strife in Cuba continues without any marked change in the relative advantages of the contending forces. The insurrection continues, but Spain has gained no superiority. Six years of strife give the insurrection a significance which cannot be denied. Its duration and the tenacity of its advance together with the absence of manifested power of repression on the part of Spain cannot be controverted, and may make some positive steps on the part of other Powers a matter of self-necessity."

Here we have a clear case of an imbecile personage unable to transact its affairs or keep its establishment in order, for whom a committee must somehow be obtained to put an end to the general inconvenience caused by the existing state of affairs.

The conclusions which we draw from the whole matter are that in the natural life of the body of States certain occasions occur at frequent intervals in which intervention by one or more States in the affairs of some other member of that body becomes a duty either (1) directly for the welfare of that member or (2) for the general good of the intervening State. As regards the second case, the remarks we have made as to intervention to preserve the balance of power necessarily include the case in which a State intervenes to prevent the balance being upset by its own partial or total extinction. As regards the first two cases they are capable of being classified under the heads of (a) minority, (b) senile incapacity, (c) lunacy of various degrees, (d) criminality, (e) prolonged bankruptcy, (f) general barbarism of polity, *e.g.* Turkey or India. This is an analogous case to minority.

Having thus stated our view of the theory of intervention among States, we now proceed to give a brief conspectus of the interventions of the last century, and to shortly state under what head each of them ranges itself naturally according to our theory :—

GROUP A.

Restraint on Dangerous Lunatic States.
1. Great Britain, Russia, Prussia, and Austria in Turkey, 1840.
2. Powers in China, 1900.

GROUP B.

Meddlings in the affairs of minor States from "indirect" motives, and with no just reason.
1. Austria in Naples, 1820.
2. France in Spain, 1820–2.
3. Austria in Italy, 1831–2.
4. Russia in Turkey, 1833.
5. Austria in Italy, 1849.
6. Russia in Hungary, 1849.
7. France in Mexico, 1861.

GROUP C.

1. England in Portugal, 1826.
2. Great Britain, Russia, and Austria in Greece, 1827.
3. Great Britain and France in Holland and Belgium, 1830–32.
4. Quadruple alliance. Intervention of Great Britain and France in Spain and Portugal, 1834.
5. Intervention of Great Britain, Russia, Prussia, and Austria in Turkey, 1840.
6. Intervention of France and Great Britain in Turkey, 1854.
7. Intervention of the Great Powers in Turkey in 1877 with regard to Bosnia, the Herzegovina, etc.

All the cases in this group have one feature in common. The interventions were undertaken on behalf of minor States in different stages of weakness, imbecility, and decay, and in every case it is arguable that the intervention was in the main for the benefit of the State in the affairs of which it occurred, and was salutary in its effects on that State.

THE BURNING OF BOER FARMS AND THE BOMBARDMENT OF COAST TOWNS.

THE British nation has now been an unwilling spectator through many long and weary months of two most disquieting things. It has seen the expense of an untold amount of its gold on the war without any conclusive result, and it has seen the expense of that which is infinitely more valuable than money, viz. of the lives of the men who have "behaved like heroes in the field and like gentlemen elsewhere." Inasmuch as the author believes that the first of these things is about as irritating and the second as shocking as anything a nation could be forced to contemplate, it has occurred to him that a few words about what he is convinced is the root of the evil may possibly have some effect. On page 11 of the essay on Cromwell will be found a footnote concerning the burning of Boer farms and the insane leniency of our military staff in the present war to the Boer inhabitants. The graves of many a poor private, treacherously sniped by the people whose farms he was forced to spare and whose weapons he could not seize, bear witness to its truth.

Why does the war still drag on and why are our soldiers' lives and our guineas still being poured out? Because the English military staff headed by the Commander-in-chief have deliberately allowed the Boers to retain several thousand effective bases for supplies and information all over the country in the shape of farmhouses. Orders of ridiculous stringency, much more suitable for a regiment quartered in Manchester than in Pretoria, were issued whereby the poor, ragged, underfed private was forced either to go half-starved or to pay the rascally Boer farmers' wives famine prices for their food. What happened as soon as the British backs were turned upon the farms thus religiously respected? Precisely that which any level-headed English grocer would have foreseen though it was hidden from the society officer. Boer blood was naturally thicker than water and the Boer women were naturally tarred with the same brush as were the Boer men. Consequently they always made haste, when the British were gone, to communicate with the Boer warriors and to supply them with food, clothing, comfort and information of the best kind. Untroubled by scruples of honour, which they did not even understand, the women thus were enabled first to make heavy profits out of the English soldiers and then to render most substantial assistance in shooting them down. Why did our staff allow this ghastly farce to go on, a farce which would have made Lord Nelson, humane and generous warrior though he was, turn in his grave if he could have heard of it? Because Lord Roberts and the rest of them had imbibed the "modern view" of modern jurists and philanthropists (*vide* Professor Holland below), which is that "private property is inviolable by a belligerent," and that "war operations should be confined to combatants only." No more pernicious nonsense has ever been put forward. The ultimate basis of war is private property. War is a plant which must wither unless it is nourished by the soil of private property. Enemy combatants and non-combatants are absolutely one in spirit and they will help each other in every possible way whenever they can. The result of this weak-kneed philanthropy is before our eyes as we write, for the Boers thus abetted and supplied by their "non-combatant" relatives have on May 31, 1901, killed and wounded

174 British soldiers at Vlakfontein. If we wish to appreciate the gravity of this error let us think of the gallant young British private sent to his grave in the prime of life and leaving a destitute family behind him solely by reason of —— the theories of Mr Stead and Mr Morley and the like. Aphorisms by English soldiers, such as we set out below, to the effect that "the whole art of war is to strike at one's adversary wherever and however one can," etc. etc., are plentiful, yet in practice "the whole art of war" has been most disastrously neglected in Africa. If we wish to destroy the Boer resources let us destroy the fountain-heads from which they draw them.

The Dutchman P. S., in his remarkable letter to the *Times* of May 31st, says, "What is to be gained by prolonging our resistance *although we may get supplies of men, arms and ammunition from pseudo-royalists?*" When and to what extent may private enemy property be destroyed in war? That is the question which forms the common element in the two topics discussed in this essay. The only real limit to this destruction of which we know is supplied by instincts of common humanity and by nothing else. If our generals had proposed to bombard the Boer farms with the families inside there would have been a natural and proper outcry, but destruction of property which cripples an enemy without loss of life is quite another matter.

In the year 1882 an article appeared in the pages of the *Revue des deux Mondes* by Admiral T. Aube on naval warfare in the future. The article, which was prolix and dull and lacking in the French *esprit* which is usually conspicuous by its absence in French works of this kind, obtained a certain notoriety in England from the writer's suggestion that the best plan in a future naval war with this country would consist in either bombarding our undefended coast towns or in holding them mercilessly to ransom. Later in the same essay this prospect had so exhilarating an effect on the spirits of Admiral Aube that he executed a sort of literary war-dance in anticipation of the time when "the shores of England shall be insulted and her ports burnt."

Now, although no one is probably better aware than the naval authorities of this country that the said insulting of our shores is not likely to occur under the leadership of men of vain verbose effervescence such as Admiral Aube and the Dreyfus Generals, the naval manœuvres of 1888 made it clear that the Admiral's proposals had produced reflection in them. For during those manœuvres Admiral Tryon treated Liverpool in the proposed manner by extorting a million under threat of bombardment, while Ardrossan, Greenock, Campbeltown, and Aberdeen were treated by the *Spider* and *Calypso* in similar fashion.

Thereupon Professor Holland of Oxford University, who had not studied his "Hall" on International Law for nothing, wrote to the *Times* and called these acts "naval atrocities." The floodgates of correspondence were now opened and a cascade of common sense from the pens of grim and sometimes humourous Admirals and warriors descended on the Professor's head. Before commenting briefly on the salient facts unearthed by that controversy a word of ex-planation is necessary.

The question of the legality of bombarding unfortified coast towns in maritime warfare is bound to assume great importance to the inhabitants of the British Isles in our next naval war, owing to the number of such towns which exist on our shores.

It has transpired that in 1878, when war was on the point of breaking out between Russia and this country, the Russian fleet at Vladivostock was under orders to proceed to our undefended Australian ports as soon as hostilities commenced and to either lay them under heavy contribution or bombard them if they refused to pay up. Following on this significant disclosure we find the French Admiral Aube advocating the same plan with regard to the coast towns of the British Isles in the event of a war between France and England. His remarks were followed by a chorus of other writers in the same strain in the *Nouvelle Revue*, etc. with scarcely a single dissenting voice, and the French Government by their conduct subsequently identified themselves with Admiral Aube's opinions, for they appointed him Minister of Marine to superintend the construction of vessels specially adapted for this kind of warfare. (Hall, *Int. Law*, 4th Ed. p. 449.)

In view then of this unmistakable evidence of the intentions of two of the Powers of Europe, it behoves us to look the matter in the face and to see whether there is necessarily anything unreasonable or barbarous in it.

The subject is closely connected with two important topics of International Law, viz. with (1) "The right of devastation" in time of war, and with (2) The right of a belligerent to levy supplies in an enemy's country.

Mr W. E. Hall's views concerning these two questions lead him to the conclusion that the practice by war vessels of extorting sums of money from the coast towns under threat of bombardment would be barbarous and illegal.

"Some naval officers of authority," he says, "are disposed to ravage the shores of a hostile country and to burn or otherwise destroy its undefended coast towns; on the plea, it would appear, that every means is legitimate which drives an enemy to submission. It is a plea which would cover every barbarity that disgraced the wars of the seventeenth century. That in the face of a continued softening of the customs of war it should be proposed to introduce for the first time[1] into modern maritime hostilities a practice which has been abandoned as brutal in hostilities on land is nothing short of astounding."

---

[1] There has been one previous instance, viz. the bombardment of Valparaiso by Nunez.

It will be the object of this essay to show that the premises of Mr Hall's argument are unsound and that his objections to the practice (although such is rarely the case with so clear-headed a writer) are pedantic and bordering closely on the ridiculous.

Later on he explains that he chiefly objects on account of "the accompanying slaughter of unarmed populations."

Two great fallacies are contained in these statements.

The first lies in the supposition that any such "slaughter of the unarmed" is necessarily involved in the practice. It is extraordinary that Mr Hall should have fallen into this error in view of a fact that he himself mentions, viz. that in the naval manœuvres of 1889 the inhabitants of Peterhead were allowed two hours' grace before the proposed bombardment.

The object of the practice is destruction of the *buildings*, not of the *people* of the town. What conceivable reason could prevent the inhabitants of Peterhead from utilizing the two hours' grace to retire inland out of range?

If the people are allowed a proper time in which to flee, there is no reason why any of them should be slaughtered. As a matter of fact at the bombardment of Valparaiso by Nunez, mentioned above, the inhabitants were given a day's notice with the result that not a single man, woman or child was killed on that occasion.

The second fallacy consists in supposing that the practice of devastating unarmed towns has been "abandoned as brutal in hostilities on land."

It may be true that a land force in modern times does not devastate an unarmed town except for strategic purposes. If the town refuses to pay a contribution, there is no need to devastate it, for the invaders obtain what they want by seizing the persons and the property of the inhabitants. That no motives of humanity would prevent a land force from destroying the town buildings to exact a contribution if it suited its purposes is shown by the following conclusive fact.

P.

7

During the siege of a town by a land force it is still customary (as was shown again and again in the Franco-German War) to bombard the dwellings of the unarmed inhabitants (and to kill the latter thereby) in order to put pressure on the garrison. Even the "Institut de Droit International," which usually embodies in its rules the most humane views of the day, permits this practice in its *Manual of the Laws of War* with the proviso that buildings containing "malades et blessés" shall be respected. The manual is silent as to the slaughter of non-combatants involved in the practice.

So much for the operations of land forces. The essential difference between the bombardment of coast towns by a naval force and the corresponding act by a land force consists in the fact that in the former case only the *property* of non-combatants need be destroyed whereas in the latter case the inhabitants are like mice in a trap and many of them lose their lives. What is the object of war? To conquer one's enemy by sapping his resources and putting stress upon him. Some sapping methods are prohibited because of their barbarity. Can any one doubt whether the promiscuous bombardment of the inhabitants of Paris is not more barbarous than the destruction of the buildings of an empty commercial coast town?

Hall's and Dana's remarks on the capture of private property at sea are very relevant to the present case.

"Is the practice harsher in itself than other common practices of war; or if it be not so, is it harsher in proportion to the amount of stress which it puts upon an enemy and so to the amount of advantage which a belligerent reaps from it?" The question hardly seems worth answering.

Dana says, "It takes no lives and sheds no blood. It damages the common course of commerce and saps the strength of the enemy."

If we consider the amount of stress which would be put

upon this country by levying enormous contributions from such a commercial coast town as Liverpool, which is, one might say, the very eye of the North of England, or else by laying it in ruins, it is hopeless and ridiculous to suppose that a hostile naval force would refrain from such measures (if it ever had the chance) on account of a supposed barbarity to non-combatants which does not exist.

Mr Hall's arguments against the practice savour strongly of "bookish theoric" and not of common sense. It is also evident (as we shall show) that he was himself more than half-conscious of the fact.

His main reasons really amount to this—"Contributions are not requisitions; in levying contributions a naval force is bound to imitate a land force exactly." This argument entails a good deal of absurdity.

Contributions are supposed to be "such payments in *money* (by the inhabitants to an invader) as exceed the produce of the taxes."

Requisitions, on the other hand, "consist in the render of *articles* needed by the army, such as food, clothes, horses, etc." by the inhabitants.

We trust that the difference between these two classes of supplies from the standpoint of the inhabitants will be as self-evident as Mr Hall appears to believe.

He begins by propounding two questions:

1. Whether contributions and requisitions can legitimately be levied by a naval force under threat of bombardment without occupation being effected by a force of debarkation.

2. Whether the bombardment and devastation of undefended towns and the accompanying slaughter of unarmed populations is a proper means of carrying on war.

We have already dealt with the second query, and if our remarks have been well founded it would appear that such bombardment *is* a proper means of carrying on war, since it drains the resources of the enemy heavily without the slaughter of non-combatants.   As to the first query, Mr Hall remarks that requisitions may be quickly disposed of.

It is satisfactory to hear that " It is only in exceptional and unforseen circumstances that a naval force can find itself in need of food or of clothing." Dealing with requisitions of *stores* the writer proceeds, " A naval force can unquestionably demand to be supplied wherever it is in a position to seize. In such circumstances it would be almost pedantry to deny a right of facilitating the enforcement of the requisition by bombardment or other means of intimidation." By these words Mr Hall shows as we have observed above that he was really aware of the inconsistency of his remarks on contributions which follow.   If a naval force can, as he admits, enforce a requisition effectually by bombardment, where is the need for any " position to seize " ? The power of destruction answers the same end as the power to seize.

Contributions on the other hand he says "do not find their justification in the necessity of maintaining a force in an efficient state.   They must show it either in their ' intrinsic reasonableness ' or in the identity of the conditions with those which exist when contributions are levied during war upon land."   Why ?

" Such identity does not exist on land.   If the contributions were not paid the enemy could seize its equivalent and so accepts a composition for property which his hand already grasps."   This style of reasoning forcibly recalls that of the continental jurists who proposed to deter blockade-running by a warning " annotation " on the ship's books (see p. 37 of this volume).   Let us consider the actual position of the citizen in the case of a land requisition and of a naval one. In the first case he pays up under the threat of losing his personal property, and in the second case he pays up under the threat of losing his real property (*i.e.* of having his house knocked down about his ears).

It is true that in the second case the enemy does not seize the realty, but the all-important fact is that in each case the owner loses his property if he does not pay.

"This," the writer continues, "is a totally different matter from demanding a sum of money under penalty of destruction from a place in which he is not, which he probably dare not enter, which he cannot hold even temporarily and where consequently he is unable to seize and carry away; and *ability to seize* and the further ability, which is also consequent upon actual presence in a place, to take hostages for securing payment are indissolubly mixed up with the right to levy contributions; because they render needless the use of violent means of enforcement." This is an entirely imaginary distinction. In the first case the belligerent says, in effect, to the citizen, "If you do not pay the contribution, I shall seize your chattels, your mayor and your sons." In the second case he says, "If you do not pay, I shall knock down your dwelling-house, your town-hall and your commercial buildings." Is there any conceivable difference in the nature of the two sanctions? Each of them may be equally relied on to produce a powerful effect on the civic imagination, for in each case the owner loses his property.

"If devastation and the slaughter of non-combatants," Mr Hall goes on, "had formed the sanction under which contributions are exacted, contributions would long since have disappeared from warfare upon land." We hope that this is true, but Mr Hall overlooks the fact which we have already pointed out that there is no more need to slaughter non-combatants in levying contributions by a naval force than in such levies by a land force. The writer then repeats his assertion that the conditions for levying contributions by a naval force must be the same as in a levy by a land force.

"An undefended town may fairly be summoned by a vessel on a squadron to pay a contribution. *If it refuses a force must be landed.* If it still refuses, like measures may be taken with those which are taken by armies in the field. The enemy must run his chance of being interrupted precisely as he runs his chance when he endeavours to levy contributions by means of flying columns."

This is a very likely story indeed. Why on earth should the sailors be required to go and risk their skins on shore by imitating the movements of a flying column, when they possess all the while the means of putting pressure on the inhabitants as effectually as any flying column could do it without leaving their ships? The writer then concludes, "A levy of money made in any other manner than this is not properly a contribution at all. It is a ransom from destruction. If it is permissible, it is permissible because there is a right to devastate and because ransom is a mitigation of that right." As long as the object of war is to put stress upon one's enemy and as long as such stress can be most effectively put upon him without any necessary barbarity to non-combatants, by either knocking down his coast towns from the sea or exacting heavy ransoms in lieu of this, so long will belligerents continue the practice, even though (as a correspondent of the *Times* observes) volumes were written to prove that it is contrary to International Law. This subject recalls an incident in the life of Nelson. After the battle of Copenhagen, when the Danes were wasting time with fruitless negotiations and Nelson was fast losing his patience, he remarked one night when going in to dinner in the King's palace that "he did not know about the negotiations but he knew that the palace would *burn well.*" Very shortly afterwards the Danes saw fit to make peace. In order to deter belligerents from such bombardments it would have to be proved as a fact that the human suffering caused by them was out of all proportion to the material damage inflicted on an enemy. Mr Hall concludes by naïvely regretting that "the officers who levied imaginary contributions during the British naval manœuvres of 1889 acted in a manner indefensible in war. At Peterhead two officers were sent in with a message demanding a large sum within two hours under penalty of bombardment; a very large sum was in like manner demanded at Edinburgh by a force which could not possibly have ventured to set foot on land." Why *should* they have ventured on land? They knew better. Whether the practice is wholly indefensible or not we feel sure that it would be far safer to make the coast towns defensible than to rely on the indefensibility of the practice.

We now return to the *Times* correspondence of August 1888, having indicated the probable source of Professor Holland's opinions regarding naval atrocities. According to our view the controversy is chiefly noteworthy for throwing a very clear light on two facts. The first of these is that as to the particular point of practice in naval warfare, which is the subject of this essay, the seamen were entirely in the right and the Professor was in the wrong. The second is that when the Admirals came to deal with the nature of International Law they blundered hopelessly and the positions were conspicuously reversed.

Professor Holland's first letter calling attention to the "naval atrocities" of the *Spider, Calypso,* etc. during the manœuvres of August 1888, was followed up by another one on August 29th explaining his views in detail, and containing, in our opinion, some very remarkable statements. There is, he says, overwhelming evidence in favour of the "modern view" that private property is inviolable by a belligerent except in certain cases, among which contributions of money are not included. We have now in S. Africa seen the "modern view" put into practice—and its results. He also says that "the general practice of the nineteenth century is against it," which in this case means no more than that no naval war occurred in that century in which the question assumed any importance. Finally he says that the *Times* naval correspondents "incline to revert to buccaneering." They did so in order to save the coast towns from what Admiral de Horsey well called a bitter awakening, in the next naval war.

One of the clearest exponents of the sailors' views was Mr Gibson Bowles. He pointed out (Aug. 31) that everywhere on land private property first suffers and most suffers, that the French in 1871 had to pay a contribution of 200 millions out of their private property, that a State cannot fire a shot without diving into private pockets for public objects, and that the final basis of the whole thing is private property. "Belligerents," he says, "do not address their energies solely to the cutting of throats." Inasmuch as a single war-ship can, according to the *Times* of August 17th, 1888, inflict losses to the amount of twenty times its own value in a few days, it is not surprising to find another *Times* correspondent on August 20th declaring that "no practical man could ever believe (viz. the illegality of bombardments), though all the theorists wrote volumes to maintain that it is the necessary outcome of International Law." Further, on August 31st a letter from H. T. M. states that in 1854 the British Fleet bombarded Odessa (practically a defenceless town) and treated Taganrog, Berdiansk and Marcopoli in the Black Sea in the same way, so that it is not even true that our own practice is against such acts. Captain James says, "The talk about International Law (forbidding the practice) is all nonsense. The whole act of war is to strike at the weakest points wherein and whatever they may be." It was also suggested that if Brighton in the future be called on to choose between contribution or bombardment it should wire to Oxford for advice in its hour of need.

Now, we are convinced, for the reasons already stated, that this practice is a perfectly lawful incident of war and that the Admirals were quite correct in holding that it will be freely resorted to in future naval contests, but we wish to emphatically protest against the views on the nature of International Law expressed by nearly all of them and by the *Times* as well. The *Times* is the most culpable of all. For we do not expect sailors to be accurate thinkers on jurisprudence, but the *Times* ought to know better. In a leader of August 17th that journal delivered itself as follows: "The rules of International Law are singularly precarious agreements observable just so long as it may suit the strongest nations to observe them and not a moment longer." That the most responsible English newspaper should use language which countenances every act of bad faith in international practice (such as that of Russia with regard to bringing war-ships into the Black Sea in 1871) and which directly asserts that might is right in International Law is nothing short of disgraceful. Moreover it is untrue. The examples of trade and of society show that the assumption is false and does not work in practice. What is the effect of unwritten law, *i.e.* of public opinion, in these two spheres of life? Is not the most unscrupulous person fettered to a great extent by it and restrained from doing many things which are not breaches of the civil law? Everyone who knows anything of commerce or society knows that this is so. That which is true of the private relations of men is true of their national relations also, though the truth is not so immediately perceptible in the latter sphere because everything is on a larger scale in it. Captain Fitzgerald says, "We have given up killing women and children not in compliance with the mandates of that *shadowy ghost* called International Law but because the growth of a higher civilization and a respect for the doctrines of Christianity have softened our savage nature and caused us to revolt against the barbarous act." Now, real genuine International Law is simply a concrete codification of the results of those feelings, and if a company of nations, as at Paris in 1856, solemnly pledge themselves to some future line of conduct, it is absurd to say that this pledge will not act as a strong deterrent against departing from that line of conduct thereafter. Public opinion is a tremendously strong factor everywhere, for man is the most imitative of all creatures. There is a popular delusion (which the *Times* most fully shares) that in dealing with the relations of companies of men, *i.e.* of International Law, all the social and psychological laws which prevail among individuals are immediately abolished. The contrary is the truth. "The State" is a fictitious personage and is merely an aggregate of human individuals with human consciences and human nerves. No such fictitious and conscienceless monster as "the State" of which the *Times* conceives has any existence.

It is against etiquette that a man should cheat at cards. Can a member of London society afford to cheat if he wishes to do so, simply because he may not be punishable by law? Great Britain paid three millions for the Alabama business because she had clearly failed in her duties as a neutral, although no power existed which could have forced her to pay the money.

The confusion about International Law has arisen through ignorance as to what it really is. Because, as Professor Holland points out, some one point of International Law is shown to be obsolete and to conflict with modern military necessities (as in the case of naval bombardments), the *Times* and its naval correspondents at once jump to the conclusion that International Law is "all nonsense" and "a shadowy ghost."

They all lose their heads over the fact that there is no petty official in International Law like the police magistrate in civil law who can fine an offender forty shillings on the spot. Yet there are still other methods *in rerum natura* than that of the forty shilling fine for punishing an offender, whether a nation or an individual.

Professor Holland points out that many people identify International Law with the writings of Vattel or of some other pedant whose writings on the subject form a maze of illogical nonsense.

Yet International Law in truth is no idle academical pedantic science. "Statesmen and diplomatists," says Holland, "prize courts, Judges, Generals and Admirals have helped to form it from their experience."

International Law is a product of eternal justice. It is not Vattel and it is not Puffendorf or Bluntschli. In spite of their nonsense and in spite of the tea-cup logic of the *Times* it exists and will exist as a hard uncompromising fact and an ever-increasing force in the life of States.

THE EXTENT OF TERRITORIAL WATERS[1].

THE following subjects are discussed in this essay :—

I. The nature of the "rights" exercised over territorial waters.

II. The theory of cannon-range as the measure of jurisdiction over territorial waters.

III. The three-mile limit.
    (α) Jurists' opinions.
    (β) Treaties and municipal regulations.
    (γ) Russian practice and admissions.
    (δ) United States practice and admissions.

IV. The incidents of jurisdiction over territorial waters.
    (α) Right of visit, search and arrest.
    (β) Alleged right of excluding foreigners.
    (γ) (1) The prohibition of fighting.
        (2) The granting of asylum.

V. Alleged extensions of the three-mile limit in the practice of nations.
    (α) For fishing purposes.
    (β) For revenue purposes.

VI. Bays and Straits as territorial or closed waters.

VII. Hot pursuit out of territorial waters.

I. and II. The subject of the right of a State to exercise control over a belt of the water which bathes its coasts may be considered conveniently from the standpoints of

    (A) Peace,
    (B) War.

---

[1] As regards the data in this essay, but not as regards the conclusions in it, the author is indebted to the labours of Mr Vesey Knox, Barrister-at-law.

It is the primary object of this paper to establish two propositions :

(1) That this right of control, whether it be proprietary or (as is submitted hereafter) merely jurisdictional in character, is in its nature a peace-right and not a war-right and that the occasions on which it becomes important are always with one exception connected with a state of peace and not with a state of war.

(2) Consequently, that it is not true that the increased range of modern artillery fire has necessitated or produced an increase (except in one case) in the width of territorial waters over which a State has hitherto been entitled by the ordinary rule of International Law to exercise control, viz., over a belt of three English marine miles from the shore.

(A) In time of peace the territorial water jurisdiction of a State is of constant importance with regard to :

(1) Protection of revenue.
    Customs and excise dues (Douane).
(2) Protection of fishing interests of various kinds and other maritime sources of wealth, *e.g.* oyster and coral beds.
(3) Navigation regulations and harbour dues.
(4) Sanitary regulations.   Quarantine.
(5) The right of a State to protect itself in time of peace from a too close or too inquisitive scrutiny of its shores and fortifications by foreign war vessels, and to prevent the approach of foreign war vessels too near its shores.

The jurisdiction of a State in these matters gives rise to the following incidents :

(*a*) The right of visit, search, and seizure of foreign vessels.

(*β*) The right to arrest and to punish all persons who are guilty of breaches of its municipal law within its territorial waters.

(γ) The alleged "right of exclusion" of foreign vessels from its waters.

As regards the extent of the territorial waters in which all the above acts of jurisdiction may be lawfully exercised, it has been the usual practice of States hitherto to make use of one common measure for them all, viz. three miles, a distance which, when first selected, was supposed to be coterminous with the extreme range of a shot from a cannon. Alleged exceptions are discussed hereafter.

(B) Considering the question of territorial water jurisdiction from the standpoint of war, we find that it only arises in one case, viz.

> The right of a neutral State to security from damage to its territory arising out of the naval conflicts of belligerents too near its shores. Dependent on this right there arises also the
>
> Right of preventing pursuit into neutral waters and of granting asylum.

Now although the original cause of the selection of this three-mile limit, viz. cannon-range (a subject which is dealt with later in this paper), is no longer the same as when it was first utilized as a measure, and although no representative international convention, such as was held at Paris in 1856, has definitely adopted the three-mile limit, yet it is thoroughly well recognized in international practice (as is shown later from the Russian and United States Governments admissions) as the extent of the territorial water jurisdiction of States for almost every case in which that jurisdiction is exercised.

As regards the lack of definite assent to this limit by the body of civilized States, it may be observed that there is an almost exact analogy between the (international) legal aspect of rules of this kind and the (municipal) legal aspect of English trade customs. A trade custom often becomes established and accepted by members of a trade for a long period before a case comes up for decision in the Courts, which causes the definite legal recognition of the custom, and the same applies to many well-recognized rules of International Law, only a very small number of which have ever been formally assented to by a representative body of civilized States. As regards the questions of

    (a) Cannon-range in relation to the three-mile limit;

    (β) The adequacy of the three-mile limit for all the purposes for which it is employed;

the following observation is necessary:

The suggestion of a three-mile limit for territorial jurisdiction as determined by the cannon-range of this day was first made by Bynkershoeck to supply the want of some such uniform measurement for the exercise of the various kinds of municipal jurisdiction which have been enumerated above.

He selected this measurement of jurisdiction as an ingenious and picturesque solution of the difficulty which secured a uniform limit for all kinds of jurisdiction with some show of reason.

It is the object of this paper to show

(1) That this theory of cannon-range as the effective cause of determining the limits of territorial water jurisdiction depended in its inception on a picturesque fiction and has depended on a fiction ever since.

(2) And that the increased range of modern artillery is not material (except in one case) to the adequacy or otherwise of the three-mile limit for the purposes for which it is now used by States.

Mr W. E. Hall says (*International Law*, p. 158), "In claiming its marginal seas as property a State is able to satisfy the condition of valid appropriation because a narrow belt of water along a coast can be effectively commanded from the coast itself either by guns or by means of a coastguard." And at p. 160 he says, "Perhaps it may be said without impropriety that a State has theoretically the right to extend its territorial waters from time to time at its will with the increased range of guns."

It is submitted that as regards the assertion of effective control over territorial waters by means of shore artillery these passages are the direct opposite of the truth.

By referring back to the cases of territorial water jurisdiction in peace and war, arranged under heads A and B, it is submitted that this can be proved as follows :—

A. (1) *As to protection of Revenue.* Although recourse is had to forcible means in this case, such means are not connected with the use of shore artillery. English revenue-cutters board vessels at a distance as great as 12 miles from the coast, but the revenue laws are not enforced by means of shore forts. Vast areas of the coast contain neither guns nor forts.

It may be urged that the paucity of guns on any given part of the coast-line is not material to the question of the possibility of jurisdiction by means of them, inasmuch as a very small number of guns would be sufficient to terrorize the owners of fishing boats and others, and that the bare chance of coming within range of guns which can be accurately used up to six thousand yards would be an effective deterrent. It may also be pointed out that, in the civilized State, there is no need for a policeman at every corner to prevent breaches of the law, and that a mere handful of them is sufficient to keep the peace in a district.

Yet, if all this be admitted, we are confronted by the following conclusive fact. For about 12 hours out of the 24 in our latitude all jurisdiction by shore artillery over any considerable belt of water is wholly determined by darkness. There is then during all this time no "sanction" at all from this source to deter the owners of foreign vessels from committing breaches of the law. An illustration from municipal affairs may be given. If all the police were compulsorily retired from duty every night, to the knowledge of everyone, it is evident that they would cease to deter burglars from crime. Jurisdiction by shore artillery is a fiction.

(2) The same is true of the protection of fishing interests.

The question of the adequacy of a three-mile fishing limit is not material here, but it must be evident to anyone who considers the matter that the " sanction " which deters foreign fishermen from fishing in English territorial waters and bays, is certainly not the fear of shore artillery. If such fishermen were to come within the three-mile limit, there is an overwhelming balance of probability that there would be no shore artillery within reach of them. The fear of English gun-boats, and of loss of license, are the causes which make foreign fishermen respect the limits of English territorial waters. If we take a liberal estimate and suppose that there are six stations between the North Foreland and Romney Marsh on the English Coast where there are guns which could throw a cannon-ball 10 miles out to sea, the absurdity of calling this alone an effective jurisdiction over a belt of 10 miles of territorial water becomes apparent.

(3) and (4) In the same way it may be shown that there is no connection between cannon-range and the jurisdiction of a State over its territorial waters, with regard to the payment of navigation and harbour dues, and to quarantine regulations.

(5) In the case of protection of coasts from foreign espionage or from the undue approach of foreign war vessels the same reasoning applies as in the case of the fishing boats.

For (i) There is an extreme improbability that there would be any coast artillery within effective range.

(ii) Even if there were, it is most improbable that it would be used against the war vessels of a State with whom the territorial Power was at peace. The idea of resorting to bombardment in such cases except on the eve of war or during war is absurd.

B. As regards territorial water jurisdiction in war. This

furnishes the only case in which the question of the improvements in modern artillery is directly involved in that of the limit of territorial waters.

There can be no doubt that modern naval guns might possibly inflict serious damage on neutral property if fired from a distance of more than three miles from land, but inasmuch as the damage would only arise in an abnormal case, viz. a naval war, there seems to be no reason why there should not be an exceptional war limit within which fighting should not be permissible.

This limit would necessarily be the same for granting asylum. On the other hand it may be urged that the likelihood of such damage when the action is fought three miles from land is very remote.

It is submitted from the foregoing examples that the question of cannon-range is only material to the question of the extent of territorial waters in one exceptional case. If it were true as Mr Hall contends that theoretically a State can extend its territorial waters with the range of its guns, the state of things in the English Channel would be most anomalous. For both English and French artillery are now capable of throwing projectiles on to the opposite coast, so that each State would now be theoretically entitled to the whole channel between Dover and Calais as territorial water.

Calvo's mistake as to the origin of the right is shown clearly by the following passages. "From these general principles it is easy to deduce that the territorial sea can only include the space capable of being defended from the land or of serving as a base of attack on its adjoining coast. Since the invention of fire-arms this space has generally been fixed at three marine miles," etc.

The fallacy of this reasoning is evident. For immediately an attack is intended on the adjoining coasts all respect for "lignes imaginaires" and theories of territorial water jurisdiction are thrown to the winds, and the attacking force attempts to take up the position best suited to its gun's range. On the other hand, the theory of defence from the land is equally absurd, inasmuch as if the occasion arose in war of effective defence of the land, no attention would be paid to imaginary belts of territorial water.

We now submit that the only right which a State possessed over its territorial waters (except as regards territorial enclaves, the entrance of which can be effectually closed by artillery) is a mere "droit de surveillance" and not a right of property. The theory of a right of property in such waters is attended by many consequent absurdities. (1) Any acts of jurisdiction with respect to it, so far from being "effective," are only exercised spasmodically and at wide intervals. When a storm arises the "property" forcibly drives its "owners" away from it. (2) The right of property would involve the right of exclusion even in time of peace, yet no sane attempt could ever be made by a maritime State to exclude the innocent passage of foreign vessels in time of peace over its territorial waters. (3) If the territorial waters really belonged to the State, it is clear that by the laws of neutrality all possibility of damage to vessels within the neutral zone in time of war ought to be excluded, so that the territorial waters being theoretically neutral territory would then require to be themselves protected by another belt of waters of equal extent. " The ocean is physically incapable of dominium."

III. (a) As regards jurists' opinions a brief reference to them will suffice. They all say nearly the same thing.

Twiss and Manning fix the limit of jurisdiction at a marine league from the shore, and the former adds that " the right of fishing in the open sea or main ocean is common to all nations."

Sir R. Phillimore says, " The rule of law may now be considered as fairly established, viz. that this absolute property and jurisdiction (in territorial waters) does not extend unless by the specific provisions of a treaty or an unquestioned usage beyond a marine league (being three miles) or the distance of a cannon-shot from the shore at low tide."

M. Calvo, p. 356, says, "Les limites juridictionelles d'un état embrassent non seulement son territoire, mais encore les eaux qui le traversent ou l'entourent, les ports, les baies, les golfes, les embouchures des fleuves, et les mers enclavées dans son territoire. L'usage général des nations permet également aux états d'exercer leur juridiction sur la zone maritime jusqu'à 3 milles marins ou à la portée de canon de leurs côtes."

The Institute of International Law ultimately adopted the limit of six miles for territorial waters inasmuch as that is the greatest distance which any European Power has hitherto proposed to claim.

Mons. Geffcken, *Revue de droit international*, Vol. 22, 1890, says : "One formerly regarded cannon-range as the limit ; but cannon-range having become uncertain by new inventions, this limit has been fixed by treaties and laws at three miles from the coast" (*vide* Art. 1 of the treaty of 11th November 1867, between France and England ; Convention of States bordering on the North Sea, 6th May 1882, Art. 2 (English) ; Customs Consolidation Act 1876; Territorial Waters Act 1878).

(β) At the Séance pleine of the Institute of International Law, held at Hamburg in December 1891, M. Aubert's report says, " Norwegians have with the other Scandinavian countries, Sweden and Denmark, the ordinary marine ' mille ' of ancient times, that is to say, the geographic league, as the extent of territorial water."

Denmark has undoubtedly adhered to the treaty of 1882 concerning fishing in the North Sea. But as M. Matzen, the eminent writer whose opinion is authoritative on matters of Danish Public Law, says (*Den Danske Statsförfatningsret*, Copenhagen, 1888, I. 36 ff.), " la règle générale du Danemark, en dehors des termes de ce traité, maintient encore l'ancien mille géographique."

According to Mr T. Barclay who acted as one of the reporters at a "commission d'étude" of the Institute of International Law :—

"The three marine mile limit seems to have been adopted by the government of the United States for the first time in 1793, when Mr Jefferson, Secretary of State, wrote to the English Minister (8th November) that the limit of a marine league had been provisionally adopted as that of the territorial waters of the United States."

In 1857 Great Britain and France agreed to a limit of three marine miles for fishing near the five Newfoundland Harbours.   In 1859 Great Britain and Russia re-affirmed by treaty the clause as to free fishing in the treaty of 1825.

In 1866 Belgium adopted a three-mile fishing limit.

In 1874 Great Britain and Germany agreed that fishing should be free except within three miles of the North German Coast or within bays of which the entrance did not exceed ten miles in width.

In 1882 Great Britain, Belgium, Denmark, France, Germany and the Netherlands agreed by treaty at The Hague that fishing should be free to all throughout the North Sea except within three miles of the coasts of any of the above States.

In 1888 the French adopted a municipal law for France and Algeria whereby fishing was only prohibited to foreigners within the three-mile limit and within bays less than ten miles wide at their entrance.

In 1891 the Belgians adopted similar regulations.

M. Calvo, Vol. 5, p. 247, quotes the Russian Regulations of 1869 (which are set out later) and adds, " Similar regulations are to be found in the Danish Regulations of the 16th February 1864, Sec. 8 ; in the Prussian Regulations Sec. 9 ; in Sec. 3 of the Austrian Ordnance of the 3rd March 1864 ; in the 4th Sec. of the French Instructions of the 25th July 1870, and in the 1st Sec. of the supplementary instructions."

Apart from the question of the adequacy of the three-mile limit of territorial water for all purposes, the following instances of Russian practice in the matter leave no doubt as to the Russian view of the custom among nations on this point.

(γ) In 1821, after the well-known Ukase of the 4th September had been published whereby foreign ships were forbidden to approach within 100 Italian miles of the Russian possessions in and around the Behring Sea, both the United States and Great Britain immediately denied the right of the Russians to exercise any such jurisdiction. Thereupon the latter explained that the measure was a defensive one and aimed at preventing the supply of arms by traders to the natives wherewith to murder the Russians in their Settlements.

By the subsequent treaty of the 17th April 1824, between the United States and Russia, the latter wholly abandoned the claims put forward in the Ukase of 1821. In the Russian customs regulations the three-mile limit is recognized.

(δ) The view which the United States have always taken of the three-mile limit is clearly set out in the following statement by Mr Seward. The note is dated 16th December 1862 : " It must always be a matter of dispute at what point the force of arms, exerted on the coast, can actually reach......
The range of a cannon-ball is shorter or longer according to the circumstances of projection, and it must always be liable to change with the improvement of the Science of Ordnance.
......A more practical limit of national jurisdiction upon the high seas was indispensably necessary and this was found, as the undersigned thinks, in fixing the limit at three miles from the coast. This limit was early proposed by the publicists of all maritime countries. While it is not insisted that all nations have accepted or acquiesced and bound themselves to abide by this rule when applied to themselves, yet three points involved in this subject are insisted on by the United States.

(1) That the limit has been generally recognized by nations. (2) That no other general rule has been accepted.

(3) That if any State has succeeded in fixing for itself a larger limit, this has been done by the exercise of maritime power and constitutes an exception to the general understanding which fixes the range of a cannon-shot (when it is made the test of jurisdiction) at three miles. So generally is this rule accepted that writers commonly use the expressions of a range of cannon-shot and three miles as equivalents of each other. In other cases they use the latter expression as a substitute for the former."

Again, on the 10th August 1863, he says, "It cannot be admitted...that the mere assertion of a sovereign by an act of legislation, however solemn, can have the effect to establish and fix its external maritime jurisdiction. His right to a jurisdiction of three miles is derived not from his own decree but from the law of nations and exists even though he may never have proclaimed or asserted it by any decree or declaration whatever. He cannot, by a mere decree, extend the limit and fix it at six miles, because if he could, he could in the same manner, and upon motives of interest, ambition, or even upon caprice, fix it at ten or twenty or fifty miles without the consent or acquiescence of other Powers which have a common right with himself in the freedom of all the ocean. Such a pretension could never be successfully or rightfully maintained."

Mr Fish also wrote (Letter of 22nd January 1875 to Sir E. Thornton): "We have always understood and asserted that pursuant to public law no nation can rightfully claim jurisdiction at sea beyond a marine league from the coast."

Again in 1887 on the occasion of the seizures of United States fishing vessels by Russia, in the "Brief for the United States" it is said, "Concerning the doctrine of international law establishing what is known as the marine league belt, which extends the jurisdiction of a nation into adjacent seas for the distance of one marine league or three miles from the shore and following all the indentations and sinuosities of its coast, there is at this day no room for discussion. It must be accepted as the settled law of nations. It is sustained by the highest authorities, law-writers, and jurists. It has been sanctioned by the United States since the foundation of the Government. It was approved by Mr Jefferson, Secretary of State, as early as 1793 and has been re-affirmed by his successors, Mr Pickering in 1796, Mr Moddison in 1807, Mr Webster in 1842, Mr Buchanan in 1849, Mr Seward in 1862, 1863, 1864, Mr Fish in 1875, Mr Ewarts in 1879 and 1881, and Mr Bayard in 1886. Sanctioned thus by an unbroken line of precedents covering the first century of our national existence, the United States would not abandon this doctrine if they could, they could not if they would."

IV. As regards the chief incidents of jurisdiction over territorial waters, viz. visit, search and arrest, it is clear that inasmuch as any extension of the three-mile limit would further extend the limit within which such acts are permissible, any such extension would be regarded with the utmost jealousy by the body of States.

V. (a) As regards alleged extensions of the limit for fisheries.

At Sec. 356 M. Calvo thus speaks of fisheries in territorial waters, "Some governments have put forward the pretension that the extent of the sea reserved for fishing for the exclusive benefit of the inhabitants of the adjacent coast should be greater than that reserved for defensive purposes, but this pretension has never been admitted as rightful. Thus, Denmark having at a certain epoch claimed the exclusive right to fish in the whole sea of Greenland, the other States, although she afterwards reduced her pretensions to the waters within 75 miles of the coast and although she contended that her rights were based on treaties, refused to respect such pretensions for the reason that as one could not acquire by usage or by treaties a property in the open sea so one could not extend territorial waters."

He continues: "If such derogations from universal principles are established, it is because they are dictated by maritime interests of great importance, notably the destruction of coast fisheries of an exceptional kind such as banks of oysters and other shell fish. Such derogations must be confined in their scope to the special object which has caused their adoption, and in order to become obligatory they must be sanctioned by express written conventions."

(β) Alleged extension of the three-mile limit for revenue purposes.

The determination of this question is of great importance in the present case for the following reason :

If it were conclusively established that it is permissible for a State to indefinitely extend its jurisdiction beyond the ordinary three-mile limit (recognized by International Law) for its private ends relating to its revenue and forcibly visit, search and seize beyond such limit the vessels of other nations with whom it is at peace without their previous assent, it is evident that there would be no safeguard against the occurrence of such acts at any distance beyond territorial waters for any private objects which the finances or caprice of governments might dictate.

Mr R. H. Dana writes as follows in the 8th Edition of *Wheaton's International Law* (Boston, 1866), p. 258, Sec. 179 :

"The war-right of visit and search extends over the whole sea. But it will not be found that any consent of nations can be shown in favour of extending what may be strictly called territoriality for any purpose whatever beyond the marine league or cannon-shot. Doubtless States have made laws, for revenue purposes, touching acts done beyond territorial waters ; but it will not be found that, in later times, the right to make seizures beyond such waters has been insisted upon *against the remonstrance of foreign States* or that a clear unequivocal judicial precedent now stands sustaining such seizures when the question of jurisdiction has been presented."

He then deals with the alleged exception to this principle in the four-league Revenue Law of the United States. "The Statute does not authorise a seizure beyond territorial jurisdiction. The Statute may well be construed to mean only that a foreign vessel coming to an American port and there seized for violation of revenue regulations committed out of the jurisdiction of the United States may be confiscated, but that *to complete the forfeiture it is essential that the vessel shall be bound to come within the territory of the United States after the prohibited act.* The act done beyond the jurisdiction is assumed to be part of an attempt to violate the revenue laws within the jurisdiction."

And again, p. 359, he says, "It may be said that the principle is settled, that municipal seizures cannot be made for any purpose beyond territorial waters. It is also settled that the limit of these waters is, in the absence of treaty, the marine league or the cannon-shot. It cannot be successfully maintained either that municipal visits and search may be made beyond the territorial waters for special purposes or *that there are different bounds of that territory for different objects*......In later times it is safe to infer that judicial as well as political tribunals will insist on one line of marine territorial jurisdiction for the exercise of force on foreign vessels, in time of peace, for all purposes alike."

Dana further quotes Dr Twiss:

"In the opinion given by Dr Twiss to the Sardinian Government in the case of the *Cagliari*, the learned writer refers to what has sometimes been treated as an exceptional right to search and seizure for revenue, beyond the marine league, and says that no such exception can be sustained as a right. He adds 'in ordinary cases indeed where a merchant ship has been seized on the high seas, the sovereign whose flag has been violated waives his privileges; considering the offending ship to have acted with *mala fides* towards the other State with which he is in amity and have consequently forfeited any just claim to his protection.' He considers the revenue regulations of many States, authorising visit and seizure beyond their waters to be enforceable at the peril of such States and to rest on the express or tacit permission of the States whose vessels may be seized."

Sir R. Phillimore says (*International Law*, London, 1879, Vol. I. p. 274, CXCVIII.):

" Both Great Britain and the United States have provided by their Municipal Law against frauds being practised on their revenues by prohibiting foreign goods to be transhipped within the distance of four leagues from the coast and have exercised a jurisdiction for this purpose in time of peace. These were called the Hovering Acts. The present English Law on the subject is contained in the Customs Consolidation Act 1876, 39 & 40 Vic. c. 36.

" Nevertheless it cannot be maintained as a sound proposition of International Law that a seizure for purposes of enforcing Municipal Law can be lawfully made beyond the limits of the territorial waters, though in these hovering cases judgments have been given in favour of seizures made within a limit fixed by Municipal Law but exceeding that which has been agreed upon by International Law. Such a judgment, however, could not have been sustained if the Foreign State whose subjects' property had been seized had thought proper to interfere" unless the seizure was an act of reprisal for similar seizures under Foreign Laws.

On the same subject Mr Hall has the following note : " A doctrine has lately been suggested to which it may be worth while to devote a few words. In the arguments laid before the Behring Sea Arbitration Tribunal on behalf of the United States it was advanced as a proposition of law that a State has a right to make enactments under which it can assume jurisdiction upon the High Seas, exercisable at an indefinite distance outside territorial waters, for the purpose of safeguarding property and of protecting itself against acts threatening invasion of interests. The laws so passed were alleged to be binding upon other nations because they are defensible acts of force which a State has a right to exert. In support of the supposed right the practice of nations was advanced in the form of 'Hovering Acts' of fishery regulations etc. It was not difficult for Great Britain to show that the laws, by which it was argued that she and other States had acted in conformity with the American pretension, were either restricted in their operation to territorial waters or were, probably everywhere and certainly in the case of the more important countries, intended only to be enforced on foreigners *subject to the assent of their own government.* The arguments from precedent therefore fell to the ground. As regards the principle involved, it will be seen later that a right of self-defensive action upon the high seas, and even within the territory of a foreign Power, undoubtedly exists; but it will also be seen that its exercise is limited to cases of grave and sudden emergency and that the very ground and essential nature of the right are incompatible with the steady and regular application of the law. Subject to the isolated practice mentioned in the text, the laws of a State can only run outside its territorial waters against the vessels and subjects of another State with the express or tacit consent of the latter."

M. Calvo, the well-known international jurist, in his *Droit International Publique,* p. 356, writes : " This three-mile limit constitutes a fixed rule which must be observed and respected except where treaties have established another one. Two or more nations are free thus to contract or extend the limit but these are acts which only bind themselves in their reciprocal relations and they cannot apply them to or much less impose them on other States (against their will)."

Mr Barclay, who took part in and reported the proceedings of the Institute of International Law at their Meeting at Paris in 1894 when the question of territorial waters was discussed, comments as follows on the subject of Revenue Claims:

" These extensions of the limit of revenue jurisdiction beyond the three-mile limit have not been confirmed as has that limit by international agreements and have not been adopted by different States in their municipal laws in a uniform fashion. There does not exist as regards them either a custom in International Law to regulate them nor any principle with regard to them on which a doctrine could be based."

VI. *As regards the territoriality of Straits.* Although it may be readily admitted that the increased range and effectiveness of artillery is here of great consequence in effectively converting some straits into territorial waters which were previously not so, since the entrance to them can now be successfully commanded where it was formerly impossible, yet even here there is a great distinction to be drawn between a peace *right* and a war *operation.* For instance the " Straits " between the two Commandorski Islands in the Behring Sea are at no place narrower than 36 miles. Now although it would no doubt be possible by means of two batteries placed at either side of the narrowest part of the strait to throw shells which would between them traverse the whole of the 36 miles, yet it is evident that no claim to jurisdiction in time of peace could be based on such a possibility although it is conceivable that in time of war the strait could be easily blocked by a few war vessels. The shore guns alone could not maintain an effective jurisdiction over the entrance.

Mr M. F. de Martens, Lib. Q. C. 1. Sec. 40, writes with regard to the appropriation of bays as territorial waters that the chief condition to their appropriation is " above all that the width from headland to headland does not exceed the ordinary width of rivers or double cannon-range." Vattel also says that " those great expanses of water to which the name of bay is sometimes given," such as Hudson's Bay, " cannot be appropriated as territorial waters."

M. Ortolan writes as follows on the subject of territorial seas :—

" Quant aux mers particulières et intérieures un droit exclusif de domaine et de souveraineté de la part d'une nation sur une telle mer n'est incontestable qu'autant que cette mer est totalement enclavée dans le territoire de telle sorte qu'elle en fait partie intégrante et qu'elle ne peut absolument servir de lien de communication et de commerce qu'entre les seuls citoyens de cette nation.......Du moment que plusieurs états différents possèdent des côtes autour de cette mer, aucun d'eux ne peut s'en dire propriétaire ni souverain à l'exclusion des autres."

Sir Travers Twiss and Mr Halleck follow Ortolan with the same views, and Mr Dana in his note to Mr Wheaton, 8th Edition, Sec. 187, says, " The making of such a claim (to close the Baltic) was the infirmity of the position taken up by the armed neutrality in 1780 and 1800, and in the Russian Declaration of War against England in 1803"; and the United States minister in 1875, at a time when Spain sought to extend her territorial waters, wrote as follows : " The United States will never concede that in the thoroughfares of commerce between Cape San Antonio and Yucatan or between the Key of Florida and the Cuban Coast the territorial waters of Spain extend beyond cannon-shot or a marine league. Considering the vast amount of property transported over these thoroughfares it is of the greatest importance to the interests of commerce that the extent of Spanish jurisdiction in these two straits should be accurately understood."

VII. With regard to what is termed the right of "hot pursuit" of a foreign vessel into the open sea for an offence committed in the territorial waters of a State, there is no doubt that such a right exists, but it is subject to the qualifications set out by Mr W. E. Hall. He says (*International Law*, p. 266) : " It has been mentioned that when a vessel or some one on board her while within foreign territory commits an infraction of its laws she may be pursued into the open seas and there arrested. It must be added that this can only be done when the pursuit is commenced while the vessel is still within the territorial waters or has only just escaped from them (see Bluntschli, Sec. 342, and Woolsey, Sec. 58). The reason for the permission seems to be that pursuit under these circumstances is a continuation of an act of jurisdiction which has been begun or which, but for the accident of immediate escape, would have been begun within the territory itself and that it is necessary to permit it in order to enable the territorial jurisdiction to be efficiently exercised."

NELSON AND THE ADMIRALTY.

EVERYWHERE on the Continent when the present Boer War is discussed all are in agreement upon one point, viz. that hardly ever before has so great an effort been made by a leading Power with so little tangible result. In other words, the world has seen an army of professional soldiers, trained and disciplined to obedience, numbering about a quarter of a million (whose personal courage has been proved to be great), flouted and set at nought for years by an undisciplined horde of some 40,000 farmers with no previous military schooling. It is in the belief that a clue to this disquieting mystery can be found in the opinions and acts of the greatest Englishman of the eighteenth or nineteenth centuries that this essay has been written. We have said above that the men were "trained to obedience," and it is a phrase on which we would lay especial stress. It was Nelson's conviction, as will be repeatedly shown later on from his own words, that the amount of obedience required of the English soldier was such as to destroy the God-given powers of judgment and election with which a mortal is endowed and to turn him into a mere stupefied automaton to carry out without reason or reflection the commands of a superior. His words on the subject are rendered the more weighty from the fact that he often in the course of his life of conflicts had to experience their bitter truth on the occasions on which he was brought into contact with the English military leaders.

His eyes were never blinded to the excellence of the rank-and-file of our army, but his experience of its leaders, whose commissions in those days were either bought or presented to them, was often, as he himself said, of a heart-breaking nature. We believe that no fact is more certain than that nations and large bodies of men (such as the public services) retain their main characteristics and *esprit de corps* for much longer periods than the lives of individuals and only change them with extreme slowness. In other words, there is a great persistency in their leading traits. For the truth of this law we would especially refer to the remarks of Cromwell on the various nations of Europe which are quoted earlier in this volume, and to the remarks of Lord Nelson, set out hereafter, on the British army, in the light of the events of the recent African War. In each case we believe that they will establish its truth.

At the outset we are bound to assert that which a couple of years ago would have made the hair of an average English Colonel stand on end, viz. that Nelson's whole career from start to finish was founded and built up on *intelligent disobedience to orders at critical moments.* Yet it is to that career more than anything else that we have owed ever since and do owe our maritime supremacy and our maritime commerce, which has been and is the backbone of our prosperity as a nation. Nelson's own rule of conduct in this matter is expressed in his own words at a critical moment during the siege of Malta, when military pipe-clay and discipline would have lost that important place to us but for him alone. " To say that an officer is never for any object to alter his orders is what I cannot comprehend. The circumstances of this war so often vary that an officer has almost every moment to consider ' What would my superiors direct, did they know what is passing under my nose ? ' But I find few think as I do. To obey orders is perfection. To serve my king and to destroy the French I consider as the great order of all from which little ones spring, and if one of these militates against it (for who can tell exactly at a distance?) *I go back and obey the great order and object, to down, down with the damned French villains.*" Whenever the spirit of his orders conflicted with " the letter that killeth," Nelson disobeyed the latter, with the result that two of the finest exploits in the annals of the navy, viz. the battles of St Vincent and Copenhagen, were won by acting against the foolish orders of his superiors in a crisis. Throughout the essay the only source from which we have drawn has been Southey's *Life of Nelson.* We have done so because it appears to us to be the work of a man who had laboured at his subject till his ideas thereon were perfectly clear and definite, and who further treated it throughout with great impartiality (except as regards the French, where he is quite destitute of it) and at times with an enthusiasm which it naturally aroused in him. His habit of constantly going to the fountain-head and letting Nelson's words tell their own story has given his book a reality and certainty which it could not otherwise have acquired.

One of the principal points, which it is our aim to elucidate here, is that the "spirit of unreasoning obedience" over which Nelson so often groaned and which has hitherto been so prevalent in our army, is a terrible evil in the practice of warfare, to say nothing of its effects on the personal character of the soldiery, which it is not humane to disregard. The incidents set out below in the life of Nelson prove this fact as clearly as the present war has proved it.

We have stated above that our object is to indicate a clue to the recent disastrous inefficiency of our arms which has laid about 50,000 of our gallant fellows in an untimely grave. Next to the "spirit of unreasoning obedience" we believe that the present War Office system, whereby a number of clerks, leading a sedentary life and wholly ignorant of practical warfare away on the wild ocean or on the mountain steeps, are put in authority over the men of action

and allowed, as we may say, to "run the war." Richard
Jefferies has indicated very clearly in *The Life of the Fields*
the great gulf that he perceived between men who were men
and people who were "merely people in black coats." If we
also would do so, let us consider the difference between
the hero whose career we have fragmentarily outlined and
the people at home who largely controlled his movements.

The national mind has been excited to the utmost and
with very good reason by the collapse of the civilian officials,
who have hitherto dominated the counsels of the War Office,
when they tried to cope with the actual hard facts of war.
Hitherto some strange idea has apparently existed that
because a man is possessed of intellectual keenness in the
management of finance (as in the case of the denizens of
the War Office and Admiralty), therefore, when they come
to deal with the pressing wants of sailors exposed to the
storms thousands of miles away or of soldiers struggling with
Boers, they will be able to grasp and cope with those difficulties
with which no one can cope without a long and stern
apprenticeship of actual campaigning or seafaring, which is
not by any means the same thing as being "in the City" in
an office.

Again we say that the incidents of Nelson's dealings with
the Admiralty set out below give us a kind of miniature
forecast of the conduct of the War Office in the South
African War. In each case there is the same official inability
to grasp the real position of the soldier or sailor in war and
to "back him up" accordingly. In illustration of this we
might refer to the famous "unmounted men preferred"
message to the Colonies, and to Conan Doyle's statement
previously mentioned, that a pocket filter would have saved
thousands of lives from the ravages of "enteric."

It is generally admitted that in the classical ages of Greece
and Rome great men of all-round excellence, who success-

fully united in their own persons the *rôle* of soldiers, advocates, and civil servants or statesmen, were of far more frequent occurrence than at the present day. We believe that the secret lies in the fact that they began their education in early manhood in the stern and often terrible school of practical campaigns, and thus when they came afterwards to the intellectual side of life and the management of affairs in the statesman's cabinet they had been so "salted" by the rough-and-tumble of real life that there was no fear that mere intellectual abstractions or mental hair-splittings or *jeux d'esprit* would divert their minds from the grasp of the facts. If our present educational system of football and cricket and rowing supplies this campaigning element to the life of our youths to some considerable extent (as we believe it does), let us not abandon it at the bidding of pedantic Continental bookworms who are ignorant of the moral determination and energy of character which are implicated in the question of "physique." There is a vast deal more truth than meets the eye in the saying of the Iron Duke that Waterloo was won on the playing-fields of Eton. If we were asked to point out the difference between English and Continental ideas which has produced the material difference between our possessions and theirs we should say that the English have a better grasp of the fact that a man ought to be a man first and an intellectual educated civil being afterwards, whereas on the Continent the very reverse is often believed and the result is that the knowledge and ideas of the intellectual person all end in smoke and non-resistance. Although it is only perceptible by occasional glimpses the fundamental truth of human existence remains, that it does not primarily or chiefly consist in thought or intellect but in *will* (including in that term the feelings and the passions), as the great German mind-student Schopenhauer has shown us. The French, as may be clearly perceived by their literature, regard "la raison" as the supreme good, yet it was mainly through contemning "la raison" and acting flatly against its dictates that Nelson destroyed their fleets.

The third point which we shall endeavour to make out is that inasmuch as we owe our greatness and prosperity to the navy more than to anything else, the amount of attention we bestow on it and especially of gratitude to the memory of its greatest son for his sufferings and death in the cause of his country is exceedingly limited. In particular, among the immense "suburban" classes around London, which are supposed to form the backbone of the nation, there exist the profoundest ignorance of and indifference to all naval life and concerns.

There is one further trait about the words of such men as Nelson and Trowbridge which should make them especially memorable to us now. They told the bare unvarnished truth about some of the nations who surround us. We do not mean that they always spoke unfavourably of them, but in some cases the bullets and the treachery and the bombardments had shattered the *couleur-de-rose* spectacles from their eyes. This is the reason why their words will seem to readers of the London daily newspapers to belong to some strange, unknown tongue. In the obsequious and formal chronicles of the doings of Continental royalties and ministers which daily fill up the newspapers, what chance is there that the sort of truth contained in the following words of Nelson and Trowbridge will ever leak out?

"In this (Danish) nation we shall not be forgiven for having the upper hand of them; I only thank God we have or they would try to humble us to the dust."

"I curse the day that I ever served the Neapolitan Government. Every man, high and low, is such a notorious villain that it is a misery to be with them."

"The West Indians are inimical to Great Britain. They are as great rebels as ever were in America, had they the power to show it."

"Now, you Corsicans, follow the natural bent of your character, plunder and revenge."

The *couleur-de-rose* habits of the English press in this matter include also the biographies published on the death of almost all well-known persons, which are nothing more nor less than a mass of gilt-edged fictions. What has this obsequious nonsense in common with the lives of men which Shakespeare wrote? Yet everyone knows that Shakespeare told the truth and that these are colourless lies. According to the English "obituary notices" the lives of well-known men all contained certain virtues of a formal and typical character, and for the rest neither vices nor passions nor misery. Even the Uncrowned King would have been handed down to posterity by the *Daily News* as a mild and virtuous follower of Mr Gladstone if he had only died a couple of years earlier, and not as the hard and truculent man of power who was master of Gladstone and the Liberal Party for years.

The remembrance of the subjection of a great English party to the dictates of a man who was avowedly the bitter enemy of our country may well drive us to recall the memory of Nelson in our search for a great public man[1].

We can imagine Carlyle writing as follows about our hero: "For there is this feature about most of the words of Nelson recorded by Southey which is most notable by us in England who are accustomed to read those illustrated weekly chronicles of the nobility in our ease and safety. They were uttered by a man who, sometimes for 800 days at a time, was living in hazard of life and constantly seeing the destruction of some of his comrades by his enemies or by the tempests of the sea. Fellow-reader, who art accustomed to seek food for thy imagination in the weekly pages of *The Etch* or *The Smear*

[1] The former popularity of Gladstone, the originator of the Boer republics and of the Home Rule scheme for Ireland, recalls a certain classical anecdote. An Athenian demagogue bade one of the citizens beware lest when the mob went mad it should tear him to pieces. The citizen bade him beware lest it should do the same to him when it came to its senses.

with its portraits of 'The Honourable Mrs Blatchingworth and her dogs' and 'The Honourable Master Doddington, aged three,' hast thou ever realised the depths of this man's life compared to such fiddle-faddle as this? If we do *not* soon realise that even in weekly art there are other things which are far nobler than tuft-hunting portraits and interviews it will be so much the more evil for our country. Ye Gods, when will the vast modern crop of ladies' journals give us some portraits and details of the life of women not because by birth or marriage they have got dresses, dogs, houses, hats, money or titles, but because they were real women and not shadows vain? Think of it, reader, think of the difference between that which is implied in the simple inscription 'Cornelia, the mother of the Gracchi' and the inscription in the weekly journals 'Lady Botchington's toilette at Punchestown Races.' And yet England also possesses her Cornelias if we only had the eyes to seek them out, for *they* are not self-conscious and they do not court the camera and the pen of the society journalist." Carlyle in *Past and Present* says that England has its dumb industrial Kings. It has its Queens also of the same genus.

We have adopted the plan throughout this essay of taking the various incidents of Nelson's life which are relevant to the above three topics and practically letting them speak for themselves on those topics, which they occasionally do with a vengeance.

With the life of Nelson before our eyes there is no need to go back to "antique" patterns of men and of ancient valour, for here we have a modern one in a modern setting which is sufficient for us.

If we wonder at the early precocity, the independence and disregard of his nominal superiors and the success of Nelson in the following incidents, we shall be better able to understand these things when we reflect that before he was five-and-twenty he had been through a series of toils and travel and war which would afford sufficient material for any modern *Iliad* or *Æneid.* " In war," said Napoleon, " men soon grow mature."

Nelson was one of eleven children and as his father was in consequence of very straitened means he decided at twelve years of age to enter the navy. This resolution was applauded by his uncle, who cheerfully remarked, " Let him come, and the first time we go into action a cannon-ball may provide for him at once." It was not as safe as starting in a " counting-house " at fifteen shillings a week. After various voyages and hardships, in the course of which he was nearly devoured by a polar bear while his ship was stuck fast in the ice within the Arctic Circle, he volunteered for the terrible expedition against the castle of San Juan in Nicaragua. Some of the "cold facts" of the affair speak for themselves. It is noteworthy in passing that the ultimate object of the expedition was to cut a canal between North and South America. " Eighteen hundred men were sent to different posts upon this wretched expedition ; not more than 380 ever returned. The castle surrendered on the 24th but it turned out to be devoid of all supplies and worse than a prison. The *Hinchinbrook's* complement consisted of two hundred men; eighty-seven took to their beds in one night and of the whole crew not more than ten survived. At length even the task of burying the dead was more than the living could perform, and the bodies were tossed into the stream or left for beasts of prey and for the gallinazos—those dreadful carrion-birds which do not always wait for death before they begin their work. Nelson himself was seized with the prevailing dysentery. The baleful conquest had to be abandoned. On his return to England he went to Bath in a miserable state ; so helpless, that he was carried to and from his bed, and the act of moving him produced the most violent pains. In three months he recovered and hastened to London to apply for employment. Yet in this state, still suffering from the fatal effect of a West

Indian climate, as if it might be supposed, he said, to try his constitution, he was sent to the North Seas and kept there the whole winter. The asperity with which he mentioned this so many years after evinces how deeply he resented a mode of conduct equally cruel to the individual and detrimental to the service." (Southey, abridged.)

It is clear that even thus early in his career he had learnt some lessons which are not included in the course of study for the " Home Civil Service."

We next come to the period of Nelson's life which he spent on the West India station as captain of the *Boreas*. It is a period full of incidents on which we would lay particular stress as bringing out alike the character of the man and the points we have mentioned earlier in this essay.

On his arrival at Antigua as senior captain on the station and second in command to Admiral Sir R. Hughes, he received a written order from the latter directing him during his stay there to obey the orders of " Resident Commissioner Montray," who had in consequence hoisted a broad pennant on another vessel by way of displaying the insignia of his authority. Nelson merely remarked, " I know of no superior officers besides the Lords Commissioners of the Admiralty and my seniors on the post list," and then promptly sent a boat and directed the pennant to be struck and returned to the dockyard. The same evening he went and dined with the Commissioner to show that he bore him no ill-feeling. Sir R. Hughes sent an account of this to the Admiralty, but the latter to their credit approved of Nelson's conduct. Then arose the more serious business about the Navigation Act. " The Americans," says Southey, " were at this time trading with our islands, taking advantage of the register of their ships which had been issued when they were British subjects. Nelson knew that by the Navigation Act no foreigners, directly or indirectly, are permitted to carry on any trade

with these possessions. He knew also that the Americans
had made themselves foreigners with regard to England, and
as they had broken the ties of blood and language he was
resolved that they should derive no profit from those ties
now. Foreigners they had made themselves and as foreigners
they were to be treated." [Editor's note. His single-minded-
ness and the clearness of his ideas as to the difference
between friends and enemies show him up in vast contrast to
some of our modern military leaders with their lukewarm
methods in the African war.]

"If once," said he, "they are admitted to any kind of
intercourse with our islands, the views of the loyalists in
settling at Nova Scotia are entirely done away, and when
we are again embroiled in a French war, the Americans will
first become the carriers of these colonies and then have
possession of them. Here they come, sell their cargoes for
ready money, go to Martinico, buy molasses, and so round
and round. The loyalist cannot do this and consequently
must sell a little dearer. The residents here are Americans
by connection and by interest and *are inimical to Great
Britain. They are as great rebels as ever were in America,
had they the power to show it.*"

The incidents which now follow are such an admirable
example of the treatment of zeal and enthusiasm at the
hands of Government officials that we make no excuse for
setting them out verbatim.

Nelson went with Collingwood to Sir R. Hughes, the
Commander-in-Chief, and respectfully asked him "whether
they were not to attend to the commerce of the country
and see that the Navigation Act was respected—that appear-
ing to him to be the intent of keeping men-of-war upon this
station in time of peace." Sir R. Hughes replied *he had no
particular orders, neither had the Admiralty sent him any Acts
of Parliament.* But Nelson made answer that the Navigation
Act was included in the Statutes of the Admiralty with

which every captain was furnished, and that Act was directed
to admirals, etc. to see it carried into execution. Sir Richard
said he had never seen the book. Upon this Nelson produced the Statutes, read the words of the Act and apparently
convinced the Commander-in-Chief that men-of-war as he
said "were sent abroad for some other purpose than to be
made a show of." Accordingly orders were given to enforce
the Navigation Act.

"General Sir Thomas Shirley was at this time Governor
of the Leeward Islands, and when Nelson waited on him to
inform him how he intended to act and upon what grounds,
he replied that 'old generals were not in the habit of taking
advice from young gentlemen.' 'Sir,' replied Nelson, 'I am
as old as the Prime Minister of England (Pitt the younger)
and think myself as capable of commanding one of his
Majesty's ships as that Minister is of governing the State.'"
[Editor's note. It would have been well for the finances of
our unfortunate country if the Minister *had* been as good
in his department as Nelson was in his. It might have
saved the eight hundred millions which Pitt's policy of "mere
showers of guineas" (as Carlyle called it) in Austria cost this
country.]

"The Americans were emboldened by the support they
met with (from Hughes, Shirley, etc.) and resolved to resist
his orders, alleging that the king's ships had no legal power
to seize them without having deputations from the customs.
The planters were to a man against him; the governors and
the presidents of the different islands, with only a single
exception, gave him no support, and the admiral, afraid to
act on either side yet wishing to oblige the planters, *sent him
a note advising him to be guided by the wishes of the President
of the Council.*"

"Scarcely a month after he had shown Sir R. Hughes the
law and, as he supposed, satisfied him concerning it, he
received an order from him, stating that he had now obtained

good advice upon the point and the Americans were not to
be hindered from coming and going freely if the Governor
chose to permit them.   An order to the same purport had
been sent round to the different governors and presidents ;
and General Shirley and others informed him, in an authoritative manner that they chose to admit American ships as
the Admiral had left the decision to them.   These persons,
in his own words, he soon 'trimmed up and silenced,' but
it was a more delicate business to deal with the Admiral.
'I must either,' said he, 'disobey my orders or disobey
Acts of Parliament.   I determined upon the former, trusting
to the uprightness of my intentions and believing that my
country would not let me be ruined for protecting her
commerce.'   Then he wrote to Hughes respectfully declining
to obey till he had had an interview with him.   Sir Richard's
first feeling was that of anger, and he was about to supersede
Nelson ; but having mentioned the affair to his captain, that
officer told him he believed all the squadron thought the
orders illegal and therefore did not know how far they were
bound to obey them.   (Nelson's spirit was apparently con-
tagious.)   It was impossible therefore to bring Nelson to a
court-martial composed of men who agreed with him on the
point in dispute."

After Nelson had proceeded to put the Act into execution
by seizing some of the ships we find that "this raised a
storm ": the planters, the custom-house, and the Governor
were all against him.   Subscriptions were opened and pre-
sently filled, for the purpose of carrying on the cause in
behalf of the American captains ; *and the Admiral, whose
flag was at that time in the roads, stood neutral.*

Prosecutions were now commenced against Nelson, the
damages were laid at £40,000, and Nelson was obliged to
keep close on board his own ship lest he should be arrested
for a sum for which it would have been impossible to find
bail.   Eight weeks he remained under this state of duress.

Then the four ships he had received were condemned, and after he had memorialised the king he received the sanction of Government and approbation for his conduct. The usual touch of the ridiculous in all human affairs was supplied by the fact that the Treasury transmitted thanks to Sir R. Hughes *for his activity and zeal in protecting the commerce of Great Britain.*

"Had they known all," said Nelson, "I do not think they would have bestowed thanks in that quarter and neglected me. I feel much hurt that, after the loss of health and risk of fortune, another should be thanked for what I did *against his orders.* I either deserve to be sent out of the service or at least to have had some little notice taken of what I have done."

Nelson next turned his attention to the wholesale robberies of vast sums of the public money committed by "contractors, prize agents and others in the West Indies connected with the naval service." It may truly be said that the history of this incident in his career is about as good an instance of the fact that "virtue is its own reward" as could be found in human literature. The whole story would have formed a capital chapter in "Candide on Optimism."

The treatment his zeal received was *pour encourager les autres* with a vengeance. By way of reward for discovering among other items that Government had been defrauded of £500,000 at Antigua, £300,000 at St Lucia, £1,000,000 at Jamaica, etc., on his return to England in precarious health he and his ship were immediately sent to the Nore from June to November that the latter might serve as "a slop and receiving ship" through the exertions and political influence of the gang of thieves which he had unearthed. Afterwards it was only through the personal efforts of Lord Howe that Nelson was dissuaded from resigning his commission. "When he was first left with the command and bills were brought him to sign for money which was owing for goods purchased for the navy, he required the original voucher, that he might examine whether the goods had been purchased at the market price; but *to produce vouchers would not have been convenient, and therefore was not the custom.* Upon this Nelson wrote to Sir Charles Middleton, then Comptroller of the Navy, representing the abuses which were likely to be practised in this manner. The answer which he received seemed to imply that the old forms were thought sufficient, and thus, having no alternative, he was compelled with his eyes open to submit to a practice originating in fraudulent intentions....Nelson examined the books and papers and was convinced that Government had been most infamously plundered. These accounts he sent home to the different departments which had been defrauded, but the peculators were too powerful and they succeeded not merely in impeding inquiry but even in raising prejudices against Nelson at the Board of Admiralty, which it was many years before he could subdue."

The treatment which Nelson received in the end over this business is more ludicrously suggestive that it was *pour encourager les autres* than anything we have ever read. After he had left his "slop and receiving ship" Southey says that "he renewed his attack upon the peculators with fresh spirit. He had interviews with Mr Rose, Mr Pitt and Sir Charles Middleton, to all of whom he satisfactorily proved his charges. His representations were attended to, and every step which he recommended was adopted; the investigation was put into a proper course, which ended in the detection and punishment of some of the culprits; an immense saving was made to Government and thus its attention was directed to similar peculations in other parts of the colonies. But it is said also that *no mark of commendation seems to have been bestowed upon Nelson for his exertions,* and it is justly remarked that the spirit of the navy cannot be preserved so effectually by the liberal honours bestowed upon officers when they are worn out in the service as by an attention to those who, like Nelson at this part of his life, have only their integrity and zeal to bring them into notice."

"Not being a man of fortune," he said, "was a crime which he was unable to get over, and therefore none of the great cared about him." He shortly afterwards proved the truth of this, for when the dispute arose over Nootker Sound and the Duke of Clarence recommended him to the second Lord Chatham, Pitt's elder brother, he seems to have been as blind to Nelson's previous services and extraordinary merits as his famous brother, for he took no notice of the recommendation. Consequently we are not surprised when Southey ingenuously informs us that "the fleet had been greatly neglected during Lord Chatham's administration at the Admiralty and it did not for some little time feel the beneficial effect of his removal. Lord Hood had gone home to represent the real state of affairs, and solicit reinforcements adequate to the exigencies of the time and the importance of the scene of action. But that fatal error of underproportioning the force to the service—that ruinous economy which, by sparing a little, renders all that is spent useless—infected the British councils; and Lord Hood, not being able to obtain such reinforcements as he knew were necessary, resigned the command." [Editor's note. The mention of ruinous economy recalls memories of antique artillery in Africa.]

"What they can mean by sending Admiral Man with only five sail of the line," said Nelson, "is truly astonishing; but all men are alike, and we in England do not find any amendment or alteration from the old Board of Admiralty. They should know that half the ships in the fleet require to go to England and that long ago they ought to have reinforced us."

We now come to the occasion on which Nelson lost an eye in the service of his country. The incident is marked by two most usual features in his career, viz. by his own

indifference to the injury (for he only took *one day* off duty
for it), and by the indifference of the authorities to him, since
his services were, by a strange omission, altogether overlooked
and his name was not even mentioned in the list of wounded.
This was not the Admiral's fault for he sent home to Government Nelson's journal of the siege, that they might fully
understand the nature of his exertions. The fault was in
the Administration, not in Lord Hood. Nelson felt himself
neglected. " One hundred and ten days," said he, " I have
been actually engaged, at sea and on shore against the
enemy; three actions against ships, two against Bastia
in my ship, four boat actions, and two villages taken, and
12 sail of vessels burnt. I do not know that anyone has
done more....I have never been rewarded, and, what is more
mortifying, for services in which I have been wounded others
have been praised, who at the time *were actually in bed, far
from the scene of action.*"

During his four months' land service in Corsica in the
course of which he had lost his eye, he had also lost all his
ship furniture owing to the movements of a camp. Upon this
he wrote to the Secretary at War, briefly stating what his
services on shore had been, and saying he trusted it was not
asking an improper thing to request that the same allowance
might be made to him which would be made to a land officer
of his rank, which, situated as he was, would be that of a
brigadier-general; if this could not be accorded, he hoped
that his additional expenses would be paid him. The answer
which he received was that " No pay had ever been issued
under the direction of the War Office to officers of the navy
serving with the army on shore."

This incident affords an excellent illustration of the folly
of putting such men as Nelson (as regards their financial and
service affairs) under the control of a set of pedantic clerks
with no practical experience of campaigning. Red tape and
routine are all very well in their way, but when official hair-

splitting prevents the recompense of an unfortunate sailor for property destroyed in the service of his country, because he does not happen to be a *soldier*, the absurdity is at once manifest.

Let the reader judge from the following anecdote whether this evil has affected South African affairs. Hundreds more could be supplied if wanted. " In this war we have all been in the hands of a lot of clerks," said a stalwart officer in our hearing. He was an excellent sportsman, not yet middle-aged and sound in wind and limb. " For six mortal months," he went on, " I hung about that War Office offering to pay my own expenses out or do anything if they would send me to help in the fighting. At last I told them that it would pay them to send me out because if I were killed they would not have to pay my pension. But it was no good. Our member was afraid to say anything about it, as I desired, in the House."

Nelson now had to cooperate with General de Vins, a general of the forces of Pitt's friends the Austrians. It was heart-breaking work. We have the spectacle of Nelson urging action and of the Austrian manœuvring for inaction. Nelson urged him to take up his position at San Remo as headquarters for magazines of every kind so that he could turn his army to eastward or westward. If they only had possession of this bay they could blockade Nice. General de Vins temporised. Now follows a luminous little commentary on Pitt's passionate policy of financing Austria. " Nelson now began to suspect," says Southey, " that both the Austrian Court and their general had other ends in view than the cause of the allies." " This army," said he, " is slow beyond all description, and *I begin to think that the Emperor is anxious to touch another four millions of English money.* As for the German generals, war is their trade, and peace is ruin to them ; therefore we cannot expect that they should have any wish to finish the war. The politics of courts are so mean that private people would be ashamed to act in the same way; all is trick and finesse, to which the common cause is sacrificed." Mr Carlyle has remarked on Pitt's policy that it was a case of "Thank you for nothing—and for 800 millions of debt." We begin to think that Nelson and he were not far wrong.

The recorded words of Nelson are in particular note-worthy and remarkable, because they were usually uttered in dangerous crises and emergencies by a man whose faculties and feelings were stirred or "wound up," as it is termed, by the constant facing of death and disaster caused by enemies or by the elements.

A further light is thrown on the methods of our staunch Austrian ally and "financée" (if we may be allowed to coin a word) elsewhere in Southey's narrative. "It seems to have been Nelson's opinion," he says, "that the Austrian cabinet regarded the conquest of Naples (against which Nelson was then fighting 'tooth and nail,' Ed.) with complacency, and that its measures were directed so as designedly not to prevent the French from overrunning it. That cabinet was assuredly capable of any folly and of any baseness, and it is not improbable that at this time, calculating upon the success of the new coalition, it indulged a dream of adding extensively to its former Italian possessions and therefore left the few remaining powers of Italy to be overthrown as a means which would help its own ambitious views."

Nelson had had a somewhat unpleasant experience of the ways of an English military officer of his time at the hands of General Shirley, as we have already narrated. The rest of his experiences in that line, as detailed by Southey with perfect impartiality and entire absence of prejudice, were unfortunately nearly "all of a piece" with his first one. We now proceed to set them out in chronological order, allowing them to tell their own story. There is a strong family likeness running through them all.

1. The first incident on which we shall briefly touch is connected with the attack upon Bastia. We again quote from Southey. "Nelson had what he called a brush with the enemy. 'If I had had with me 500 troops,' he said, 'to a certainty I should have stormed the town and I believe it might have been carried. *Armies go so slow that seamen think they never mean to get forward.*' (Editor's note. Napoleon knew how to *changer tout cela.*) During this partial action our army appeared upon the heights and having reconnoitred the place returned to San Fiorenzo. 'What the general could have seen to make a retreat necessary,' said Nelson, 'I cannot comprehend. A thousand men would certainly take Bastia ; with 500 and *Agamemnon* I would undertake it.' General Dundas had not the same confidence. 'After mature consideration,' said he in a letter to Lord Hood, 'and a personal inspection for several days of all circumstances, local as well as others, I consider the siege of Bastia with our present means and force to be a most visionary and rash attempt, such as no officer would be justified in undertaking.'" Then Nelson and Hood started the siege with 1183 soldiers and marines and 250 sailors. "We are but few," said Nelson, "but of the right sort ; *our general at San Fiorenzo not giving us one of the five regiments he has there lying idle.*" The sailors dragged the guns up impossible heights and in a short time the "most visionary and rash attempt" succeeded and produced the surrender of the garrison of 4000 troops. The reader will not of course be surprised to hear that no Government notice was taken of the conduct of Nelson (who was brigadier) during the siege, but that on the contrary certain other persons were rewarded who had constantly proposed to him to get Lord Hood to abandon the siege.

When the fleet was ordered to leave the Mediterranean Nelson exclaimed, "Do His Majesty's ministers know their own minds? They at home do not know what this fleet is capable of performing—anything and everything. I lament our present orders in sackcloth and ashes, so dishonourable to the dignity of England, *whose fleets are equal to meet the world in arms*, and of all the fleets I ever saw I never beheld one in point of officers and men equal to Sir J. Jervis's, who is a Commander-in-Chief able to lead them to glory."

Before the attack on Teneriffe Nelson said, " I know from experience that soldiers have not the same boldness in undertaking a political measure that we have ; we look to the benefit of our country and risk our own fame every day to serve her ; *a soldier obeys his orders and no more.*"

2. When Captain Trowbridge acting on shore with his sailors had driven the French from the apparently impregnable fort of St Elmo at Naples by means of his naval guns formed into five batteries, Nelson wrote : "I find that General Koehler does not approve of such irregular proceedings as naval officers attacking and defending fortifications. *We have but one idea—to get close alongside.* (Editor's note. He stuck to that idea and acted on it to the death.) None but a sailor would have placed a battery only one hundred and eighty yards from the castle of St Elmo ; *a soldier must have gone according to art and the usual way.* My brave Trowbridge went straight on, for we had no time to spare."

We may here remark parenthetically that the gallant Trowbridge appears to have been one of the finest characters in the band of brothers who supported Nelson throughout his wonderful career.

Trowbridge's letters when Nelson was in the grasp of the syren at Naples form some rather pathetic reading.

"We are dying off fast for want. I learn that Sir W. Hamilton does not think it worth while to apply again to Prince Luzzi for corn. If so, I wish he commanded this distressing scene instead of me. If we cannot get the corn a short time will decide the business. I wish I was at your lordship's elbow for an hour. All, all will be thrown on you !

I will parry the blow as much as in my power: I foresee much
mischief brewing. God bless your lordship.   I am miserable ;
I cannot assist your operations more.   Many *happy* returns
of the day to you (New Year's Day), I never spent so miserable
a one.   I am not very tender-hearted, but really the distress
here would move even a Neapolitan......I curse the day I ever
served the Neapolitan Government.   We have characters, my
lord, to lose : these people have none.   Such is the fever of
my brain this minute that I assure you, on my honour, if the
Palermo traitors were here I would shoot them first and then
myself.   Oh ! could you see the horrid distress I daily experience, something would be done.   All I write to you is
known at the (Neapolitan) queen's.   For my own part I look
upon the Neapolitans as the worst of intriguing enemies :
every hour shows me their infamy and duplicity......The
whole blame will fall on you.   Every man you see, gentle
and simple, is such a notorious villain that it is a misery
to be with them."

"When the court at Naples," says Southey, "was employing
itself in a miserable round of folly and festivity, while the
prisons of Naples were filled with groans and the scaffolds
streamed with blood, Trowbridge wrote to Nelson, ' I dread,
my lord, all the feasting etc. at Palermo.   I am sure your
health will be hurt.   If so, all their saints will be damned by
the navy.   Everything gives way to the king's pleasures.' "

3.   Nelson perceiving a chance through the victories of
Suvaroff of recovering Rome and driving the French out
of Italy applied to Sir J. Erskine at Minorca to assist in
this great project with 1200 men.   "Never," said he, "was
the field of glory more open to anyone than at this moment
to you.   Rome would welcome you as her deliverer."

Sir J. Erskine's behaviour was exactly the same as on the
other occasions on which Nelson was brought into contact
with the army leaders of his country.   "Twelve hundred
men," said Erskine, "would be too few for such an under-

taking. Civita Vecchia was a regular fortress. The climate was against them. Besides he did not like to act without consulting General Fox," etc. etc. It was the same old story.

Nelson then proceeded to carry out the undertaking successfully by means of a small detachment from his fleet and of the assistance of Trowbridge.

4. He then had a further experience of Sir J. Erskine's military methods. Malta, with a garrison of 5000 French, was being besieged by Captain Ball with 1500 English and Portuguese marines and 1500 armed peasants. Ball was in desperate need of men, money, and food. Erskine would not lend any of his troops. He said that he "was expecting General Fox and could not act without orders, and that unless a respectable land force were sent against it, no hope of its surrender could be entertained, as it was one of the strongest places in Europe."

" Nelson," says Southey, "groaned over the spirit of over-reasoning caution and unreasoning obedience. ' My heart,' said he, ' is almost broken. If the enemy get supplies in we may bid adieu to Malta. *To say that an officer is never for any object to alter his orders is what I cannot comprehend. The circumstances of this war so often vary that an officer has almost every moment to consider, What would my superiors direct did they know what is passing under my nose? But I find few think as I do. To obey orders is perfection. To serve my king and to destroy the French I consider as the great order of all, from which little ones spring, and if one of these militate against it (for who can tell exactly at a distance?) I go back and obey the great order and object to down, down with the damned French villains. My blood boils at the name of Frenchman.'*" This man succeeded in his purpose.

At length Fox arrived and allowed Colonel Graham to go to Malta with means so miserably limited that Nelson actually pledged his estate of Bronté for £6000 in case there should be any difficulty about paying bills, because, as he said, "every farthing and every atom of me shall be devoted to the cause." Such was the public spirit of the man whose memory is now respectfully shelved and forgotten by us. The plain facts of his life show that it was mainly passed in the effort to arouse his apathetic countrymen to zeal in the common cause and to inspire them with the enthusiasm in that cause which possessed him and his band of empire-making sailors.

So much for Nelson and his opinion of the army of his day. We now come to the cases in which by a total but enlightened disregard of orders which conflicted with the fighting necessities of the moment he obeyed as he said the spirit and not the letter of his commands, and scored, against the rules, those splendid successes at St Vincent, Copenhagen, and elsewhere to which we owe so much of our present position in Europe.

Our extracts are of necessity condensed and somewhat fragmentary in order that they may be brief.

1. At the battle of St Vincent before the enemy could form a regular order of battle, Sir J. Jervis by carrying a press of sail came up with them, passed through their fleet, then tacked, and thus cut off nine of their ships from the main body....The admiral was now able to direct his attention to the enemy's main body, which was still superior in numbers to his whole fleet. He made signal to *tack in succession.* Nelson, whose station was in the rear of the British line, perceived that the Spaniards were bearing up before the wind, with an intention of forming their line, going large, and joining their separated ships, or else of getting off without an engagement. *To prevent either of these schemes he disobeyed the signal without a moment's hesitation and ordered his ship to be wore.* This at once brought his ship into close conflict with seven great Spanish ships. Captain Trowbridge joined in the attack with the *Culloden,* and these two vessels virtually won the battle

between them. For they were engaged with all the four ships which were captured, and Nelson took two of them practically with his own hand. He boarded the *San Nicolas* in person, and after they had secured her he actually led the boarding-party on to the *San Josef,* crying out, "Westminster Abbey or Victory!" There is no manner of doubt that he won the battle in person. The brunt of the action fell on his ship, which sustained a fourth part of the injuries of the whole action and the decisive movement which brought this about was the result of the inspiration of his genius acting in direct contradiction to his orders.

We find, accordingly, that "In the official letter of Sir John Jervis, Nelson was not mentioned. It is said that the admiral had seen an instance of the ill-consequence of such selections after Lord Howe's victory and therefore would not name any individual, thinking it proper to speak to the public only *in terms of general approbation.*"

When the action was over we learn that Sir J. Jervis received him on the quarter-deck, took him in his arms and said he could not sufficiently thank him, so that evidently at that moment of exultation he considered him worthy of something more than "general approbation." For this victory Jervis was made an Earl, while Messrs Pitt and Co. graciously consented to give Nelson the *Order of the Bath.* It should never be forgotten by Englishmen that the hero who won this battle, so to speak, wholly off his own bat, was never raised in his lifetime to the rank conferred on Jervis *as the result of Nelson's genius and exertions.*

2. When Lord Keith ordered him to repair to Minorca with his whole force, Nelson considered that it would be better to risk the loss of Minorca than that of Naples and Sicily, and therefore sent a part only of his force. He then wrote to the Duke of Clarence, "I am well aware of the consequences of disobeying my orders, but as I have often before risked my life for the good cause, so I with cheerfulness did my com-

mission; for although a *military* tribunal may think me criminal, the world will approve of my conduct, and I regard not my own safety when the honour of my king is at stake."

Later on he received a peremptory order from Lord Keith to sail for Minorca with the whole of his force. He then wrote to Lord St Vincent, "My mind, as your lordship knows, was perfectly prepared for this order; and *it is now more than ever made up.* At this moment I will not part with a single ship, as I cannot do that without drawing 120 men from each ship, now at the siege of Capua. I am fully aware of the act I have committed; but I am prepared for any fate which may await my disobedience. Capua will soon fall, and the moment the *scoundrels of French* are out of this kingdom I shall send eight or nine ships of the line to Minorca." His conduct was wholly justified by the event.

He said, when Gaeta surrendered to Captain Louis, "I am sorry you have entered into any parleying with him. *There is no way of dealing with a Frenchman but to knock him down;* to be civil to them is only to be laughed at when they are enemies." Would that in 1881 we had possessed a statesman who had acted on this truth as applied to the Boers instead of relying on sheepskin London treaties, as Gladstone did. Fifty thousand of our fine fellows are now underground because we had him not.

Nelson, by the above act, thus drove the French out of Naples. The Admiralty thought it expedient to censure him for disobeying Lord Keith's orders and hazarding Minorca without sufficient reason, and also for having landed seamen for the siege of Capua to form part of any army employed in operations at a distance (not a bad thing at Ladysmith), where in case of defeat, they might have been prevented from returning to their ships, and they enjoined him "not to employ the seamen in like manner in future."

Nelson justified his behaviour to the First Lord as follows:

"My principle is to assist in *driving the French to the devil,* and in restoring peace to mankind. I feel that I am fitter to do the action than to describe it."

3. We now come to the battle of Copenhagen, which forms, in truth, the climax among the illustrations we have already given of the stupidity of the authorities in their dealings with Nelson and of the oft-repeated fact that it was he alone and single-handed, or rather single-headed (for his sailors did his bidding like one man), who, as usual, in opposition to orders carried out that magnificent series of great naval *coups* which has secured to us the empire of the seas ever since. When the three northern courts of Russia, Sweden, and Denmark had formed a coalition to deprive England of her naval rights, and when the Baltic expedition had, in consequence, been resolved upon, Sir Hyde Parker was put over Nelson in command of the expedition by Earl St Vincent, the First Lord of the Admiralty. The results which would infallibly have followed from this appointment but for the character of Nelson we have noted later on, but we may here remark that inasmuch as (1) St Vincent owed his title to Nelson's exertions and was well aware of what he was, and (2) the only thing of note that Sir Hyde Parker had previously done had been to pave the way for the French invasion of Italy by committing the fatal error of reducing the guard at Genoa to two ships, the appointment of this personage as the senior officer of the hero of 170 fights was about the crowning act of folly concerning Nelson committed by the authorities.

We are not surprised to hear that "the public murmured at seeing the command entrusted to another." It has been "murmuring" again lately. When Nelson joined the fleet at Yarmouth he found the admiral "a little nervous about dark nights and fields of ice." Nelson said, "We must brace up. These are not times for nervous systems. I hope we shall give our northern enemies that hailstorm of bullets which gives our dear country the dominion of the sea. *We have*

*it, and all the devils in the North cannot take it from us, if
our wooden walls have fair play."*

The English Government treated Nelson with such
careless indifference that when the fleet had reached its
first rendezvous, at the entrance of the Cattegat, he had
received no official communication whatever of the intended
operations.   His own mind had been made up on them with
its accustomed decision.   "All I have gathered of our first
plans," said he, "I disapprove most exceedingly.   Honour
may arise from them ; good cannot.   I hear we are likely to
anchor outside of Cronenburg Castle instead of Copenhagen,
which would *give weight to our negotiation.*   A Danish minister
would think twice before he would put his name to war with
England, when the next moment he would probably see his
master's fleet in flames and his capital in ruins.   The Dane
should see our flag every time he lifted up his head."   Nelson
later on addressed a most characteristic letter to Sir Hyde
Parker: "Not a moment should be lost in attacking the enemy...
The only consideration is how to get at them with the least
risk to our ships.   Here you are, with almost the safety,
certainly the honour of England more entrusted to you than
ever yet fell to the lot of any British officer.   On your
decision depends whether our country shall be degraded in
the eyes of Europe or whether she shall rear her head *higher
than ever."*   (Editor's note.   Thanks to Nelson alone on *this*
occasion she did the latter.   How grateful we have been to him!)

Now comes the first occasion on which the presence of
Sir Hyde at the head of affairs all but ruined the whole
business.   There were two ways of attacking Copenhagen,
which had now become necessary in order to stop the Swedes
and the Russians from joining the Danes.   The one consisted
in passing Cronenburg and going up the King's Channel, the
other in taking the passage of the Belt.

The pilots were terrified at the thought of the batteries at
Elsinore and persuaded Sir Hyde to take the Belt way.

" Such was the habitual reserve of Sir Hyde that his own captain of the fleet (Domett) did not know what course he had resolved on till the fleet were getting under weigh." When Domett did know it, he told Parker plainly that it would ruin the expedition.   As there were only one captain and one pilot in the fleet who knew anything about the Belt passage it meant nothing but delay and accident.   Even when they were once through it the heavy ships would not be able to come over the grounds to attack Copenhagen, and light vessels would have no effect on such a line of defence as had been prepared against them.   Sir Hyde first wavered and then consented to send for Nelson, who instantly recommended the Cronenburg route.

" The Danes had profited greatly by the delay during the negotiations and a council of war was held among the British leaders as to whether an attack might be made on the terrific Danish line of ships, *radeaus*, pontoons, galleys, fire-ships and gun-boats, flanked and supported by extensive batteries and occupying from one extreme to the other an extent of nearly four miles.   Some of the members of the council spoke of the number of the Swedes and Russians whom they should afterwards have to engage as a consideration which ought to be borne in mind.   Nelson, who kept pacing the cabin, repeatedly said, ' The more the better ' (i.e. ' Let 'em all come' in modern phrase), ' I wish they were twice as many— the easier the victory, depend upon it.'   He then offered his services for the attack, requiring ten sail of the line and the whole of the smaller craft.   Sir Hyde...left everything to his judgment," which is what always happened with Nelson's superior officers whenever the real time of trial arrived.

" The next day the first great difficulty he met with arose from the fears of the pilots, who were mostly ' mates in Baltic traders.'   ' I experienced in the Sound,' said he, ' the misery of having the honour of our country entrusted to a set of pilots who have no other thought than to keep the ships clear of danger and their own silly heads clear of shot. If any merit attaches to me it was for combating the dangers of the shallows in defiance of them.' "

The bad fortune which he encountered before the battle began doubles the merit of his extraordinary performance in the teeth of adversity. " Of twelve ships of the line, one was entirely useless and two others in a situation where they could not render half the service which was required of them. Of the squadron of gun-brigs only one could get into action : the rest were prevented by baffling currents from weathering the eastern end of the shoal, and only two of the bomb vessels could reach their station on the middle ground and open their mortars on the arsenal."

When Sir Hyde, who remained in the background during the action, saw Nelson's ships under the fire of *more than a thousand guns*, which showed no signs of slackening after three hours, he evidently, putting ingenious explanations on one side, lost his head. In spite of Captain Domett's remonstrances he made the signal of recall. " The fire," he said, " was too hot, a retreat must be made." Nelson, who was drinking the delights of battle and who said that " he would not be elsewhere for thousands," turned his blind eye playfully at the signal and cried, " Damn the signal! Keep mine for *closer battle* flying. That's the way I answer such signals. Nail mine to the mast."

That Sir Hyde's panic-stricken signal might have ruined the whole action in spite of Nelson's prompt disregard of it is evident from the fact that Admiral Graves could not see what Nelson was doing and therefore had to obey or disobey it like Nelson on his own responsibility. Fortunately he shared Nelson's spirit sufficiently to disobey it, and the rest of the ships followed the example of these two. When the victory was practically won Nelson sent the following note to the Crown Prince : " Vice-Admiral Lord Nelson has been commanded to spare Denmark when she no longer resists.

The line of defence which covered her shores has struck to the British flag; but if the firing is continued on the part of Denmark he must set on fire all the prizes that he has taken without having the power of saving the men who have so nobly defended them. The brave Danes are the brothers, and should never be the enemies of the English."

As he left the *Elephant* after she had grounded on the sand he said, "I have fought contrary to orders and I shall perhaps be hanged. I don't care, let them."

We have dealt with the battle of Copenhagen at some length because incidents kept cropping up in the course of it which illustrate so forcibly the points we have previously endeavoured to set out in this essay.

For instance, after the battle, during which the only active part Parker had played consisted in attempting to stop it before a victory was gained, the British had six line-of-battle ships and eight praams as prizes. Parker caused all of them to be destroyed except one, by way of saving the trouble of sending them to England. By this act the crew of the fleet lost the prize-money they would otherwise have obtained on the sale of the prizes in England, and which they had in fact earned with their blood. Nelson was very angry. "Parker," he said to St Vincent, "*is rich and does not want the money*, but justice to the officers and men actuates me to write to you. It is true our opponents were in hulks and floats, only adapted for the position they were in, but that made our battle so much the harder and victory so much the more difficult to obtain. Believe me, I have weighed all the circumstances, and in my conscience I think that the king should send a gracious message to the House of Commons for a gift to this fleet; for what must be the natural feelings of the officers and men belonging to it to see their *rich Commander-in-Chief* burn all the fruits of their victory which if fitted up and sent to England would have sold for a good round sum?"

In accordance with the fact that it was Nelson and not the Commander-in-Chief who had fought and won the battle we next find that Nelson conducted the negotiations on shore without the assistance of that functionary. "A difficulty arose respecting the duration of the armistice. Neither party would yield and one of the Danes hinted at the renewal of hostilities. ' Renew hostilities!' cried Nelson, 'we are ready at a moment —ready to bombard this very night...' The commissioners could not agree on this point and left Nelson to settle it with the prince. A levee was held in one of the state-rooms which had been stripped of its furniture in fear of a bombardment. To a bombardment also Nelson was looking at this time ; fatigue and anxiety and vexation at the dilatory measures of the Commander-in-Chief combined to make him irritable; and as he was on his way to the prince's dining-room he whispered to the officer on whose arm he was leaning, " Though I have only one eye I can see that all this will burn well "... After dinner the prince agreed that the armistice should continue 14 weeks... Nelson saw that the temper of the Danes towards England was such as naturally arose from the chastisement which they had so recently received. ' In this nation,' said he, 'we shall not be forgiven for having the upper-hand of them ; I only thank God we have, *or they would try to humble us to the dust*'" (let the Anglo-germaniacs note this last sentence well).

Nelson was now almost bursting with impatience to go and attack the Russian fleet which was blocked up by the ice in the harbour at Revel and *lay at our mercy*. There can be no reasonable doubt that but for the indecision and delay of Parker, as Nelson himself said, " nothing could have saved one ship of them in two hours after our entering the bay." As it was, he arrived at Revel eight days after the ice had melted sufficiently to let them escape while the English were lying idly at Kioge. It is true that Nelson's terrific feat at Copenhagen had struck such terror into the breasts of the northern allies that they all hastened to make peace, but as they only did so some days later, it is clear that the appointment of Sir Hyde over Nelson did actually prevent the execution of a naval *coup* at once as brilliant and as overwhelming as any that has been achieved in the annals of our navy.

Parker was now recalled and Nelson was appointed Commander-in-Chief, but the shattered state of the health of this man of countless toils prevented his acceptance of the post. " I will endeavour to do my best while I remain," he said, " but I shall either soon go to Heaven, I hope, or must rest quiet for a time." His last impressions of the Danes are noteworthy. He saw that the Danish Cabinet was completely subservient to France and that under cover of the armistice they continued their warlike preparations against England. " I see everything which is dirty and mean going on," he says, " and the Prince Royal at the head of it. Guns are taken on board ship, floating batteries are prepared and everything is done in defiance of the armistice. My heart burns at seeing the word of a prince so falsified. Enough is done to break twenty treaties."

Those who have any curiosity in such matters will find by comparing these words of Nelson with those of Cromwell quoted in the first essay in this volume that these two great Englishmen appear to have held similar views concerning the Danish nation.

On Nelson's return to England the authorities were graciously pleased to make him a Viscount, which Southey considers "an inadequate mark of reward for services so splendid and of such paramount importance to the dearest interests of England."

It should be noted in view of recent criticism on our artillery that the *Bellona's* guns at the battle of Copenhagen turned out to be forty years old.

We shall now briefly mention one or two of the glimpses

which are obtainable in Southey's book of the terrible sufferings which this man among men went through in order to win for us our sea supremacy.   We have already mentioned the Red River expedition and the loss of his eye at Bastia, while the narrative of the final three hours of agony which he endured at Trafalgar after his backbone was shot through is too well known to be described.   Here we shall content ourselves with two other instances.

We may perhaps be permitted to call attention to the singular presentiment of his own death which possessed Nelson shortly before the battle of Trafalgar.   We have come across so many instances in which men who led lives of unusual difficulty or danger (lives, in other words, which stirred the hidden energies of the soul) have had the same feelings before death, that we here cite a few of the cases which occur to us.   Nelson went to the upholsterer who had charge of the coffin made for him after the battle of the Nile out of a French mast and told him "to have it in readiness as he should soon want it."   That great American soldier-statesman, Abraham Lincoln, on the day of his murder said at the Council of State, "Gentlemen, some evil is going to befall me to-day."   And then he told them that twice before in his life when he had had a certain dream it had been followed by heavy disaster.   "I dream," he said, "that I am alone on a wide river, and I drift and I drift and I drift."

Byron told Lady Blessington just at the end of his eventful life that he well knew he should never return from Greece.

Marshal Lannes, as he was mounting his horse on the day of Wagram, told the surgeon standing by that it would be his last fight.   Shelley at the close of his poem "Adonais" and in his letters repeatedly spoke of his death by drowning. Napoleon, when O'Meara was taking leave of him, pointed to his bed and said, "I shall die there, rongé de maladie."

Lastly we remember that a certain famous steeplechase rider, on the day when he broke his neck, unreasonably refused to take a return ticket.

But, to return to Nelson. During the great battle of the Nile Nelson received a severe wound on the head from a piece of langridge shot. Captain Berry caught him in his arms as he was falling. The great effusion of blood occasioned an apprehension that the wound was mortal. *A large flap of the skin of the forehead, cut from the bone, had fallen over one eye and, the other being blind, he was in total darkness.* When he was carried down to the cockpit the surgeon left the man under his hands to attend to him. "No," said Nelson, "I will take my turn with my brave fellows." Nor would he suffer his own wound to be examined till every man who had been previously wounded was properly attended to.... The blow had so shaken his head that from its constant aching and the perpetual sickness which accompanied the pain "he could scarcely persuade himself that the skull was not fractured."

For thus annihilating the French fleet in this battle, Pitt and his friends were pleased to create him a *Baron* with £2000 a year, and when General Walpole inquired why the lowest rank in the Peerage should have been selected, the former said, "He thought it needless to enter into that question. His fame would be co-equal with the British name," etc., etc., together with other oratorical flowers of the Pitt species.

The other glimpse concerns the time when Nelson lost his forearm at Teneriffe.

In the act of stepping out of the boat Nelson received a shot through the right elbow and fell; but as he fell he caught the sword, which he had just drawn, in his left hand, determined never to part with it while he lived, for it had belonged to his uncle, Captain Suckling.

His first letter to Lady Nelson after the amputation was as follows. " I beg neither you nor my father will think much of this mishap; *my mind has long been made up to such an event.*"

It is most refreshing to find that about this time a pension of £1000 a year was bestowed upon him.

" His sufferings from the lost limb were long and painful. A nerve had been taken up in one of the ligatures at the time of the operation, and the ligature was of silk instead of waxed thread. The ends of this being pulled every day in hopes of bringing it away occasioned great agony. He had scarcely any intermission of pain day or night for three months after his return to England....Not having been in England till now since he lost his eye he went to receive a year's pay as smart money, but could not obtain payment because he had neglected to bring a certificate from a surgeon that the sight was actually destroyed. Irritated that this form should be insisted upon, he procured a certificate for the loss of his arm, saying they might just as well doubt one as the other."

We will conclude with an imaginary dialogue between the shade of Voltaire and a modern Englishman, because it appears to us that the *esprit* of the man who uttered the epigram about the shooting of Admiral Byng (*pour encourager les autres*) would have been especially able to expose the cavalier treatment of Nelson during his life and the neglect of his memory afterwards by the English. As the shade in his lifetime was nothing if not methodical we will suppose that he touches on the events of Nelson's life in the order in which they occurred.

" I suppose," he began, "that as this zealous and invaluable young officer incurred so much odium in doing his duty over the business of the American ships at Jamaica and was practically imprisoned for it on his ship for eight weeks, something handsome was done for him on his return or at least that he was publicly thanked for his zeal." "Well, I can't say that he was," replied the Englishman, "*but Sir Richard Hughes was*, so it was all right."

The attention of the shade of the *littérateur*, who was also in life a consummate man of business, was now turned naturally to the thefts from Government at Antigua which Nelson discovered. "Surely," he began, "after this admirable officer had recovered about a million pounds for your Government through his zeal they gave him a percentage of the sum enough to form a competency for him." "No," was the reply, "the fact is that they were angry with him for doing it, and sent him on to a slop ship at the Nore for the rest of the winter, but *they gave the junior officer who succeeded him an additional allowance* and doubled the pay of the artificers in the naval yard by way of showing their gratitude." After the shade had expressed his surprise at this singular way of rewarding merit he passed on to the attack on Bastia. "But come now," he began, "these things are perhaps intelligible before Nelson was well-known to your Government. But when the poor fellow attacked and captured Bastia, as you say he did, with a greatly inferior force and got his eye knocked out in doing it, I presume they consoled him with one of your decorations of merit and a good pension." "No ; unfortunately they forgot to include his name in the list of the wounded, as it happened, but they rewarded some of the other officers. "And did these officers give Nelson much help in the attack ?" asked the shade in incredulous accents. "Well, I admit that some of them were in bed at the time," replied the Englishman, "but *no doubt they were with him in spirit.*" "Verily the ways of your Government are past finding out," exclaimed the shade warmly. The conversation then turned on the battle of St Vincent. "I suppose," he began, "that the man who practically took all my country's ships in that engagement single-handed with his own ship through so brilliantly displaying his genius and good sense in disobeying his orders to tack, was loaded with emoluments because he was successful. For I know that your countrymen worship success, although they have been known to shoot an admiral when he failed." The Englishman here showed some embarrassment, but at length he replied, "They didn't do that, but they made Jervis an Earl and gave him £2000 a year for it. But stay, I remember Nelson got something. They gave him the Order of the Bath. I suppose that they made Jervis an Earl to console his feelings because Nelson won the battle through flatly disobeying his orders. As for Admiral Byng, if he had failed nowadays my countrymen would not have shot him. They would have made him a peer and appointed him to command the Channel Squadron. Times have changed." "But may I ask whether this Order of the Bath carried any money with it?" inquired the shade of the Frenchman who said that he would give three hundred years of fame in exchange for a good digestion. "No, I cannot say that it did," replied the Englishman. "It certainly seems very extraordinary, indeed ridiculous," the shade went on, "that Jervis should have been preferred to Nelson in this way, but I suppose that after the unparalleled victory of the Nile, when Nelson dealt my country's navy a blow from which it has never yet recovered, they at least made him the equal in rank of him who was made an Earl for what Nelson did." "No, they did not," was the reply. "In fact, in his lifetime he never was raised as high in mere society rank as Sir J. Jervis was raised for the battle which was won by someone else through disobedience to his orders." Here the shade appeared to be so dumbfounded by the replies he received that he was unable to ask any further questions for some time. At length he recovered sufficiently to say, "But, come now, seriously, after this extraordinary man had altogether annihilated the sea-power of my country by his own super-

human efforts and after he had broken the sea-power of the
northern courts (which are as jealous of you now as they were
in my day) through disregarding the orders of the fool of a
commander whom they had put over him, and after he had made
the last great sacrifice of his life for his country at Trafalgar,
surely the English are at great pains to keep alive the memory
of the man who more than all others made that Empire
beyond the seas possible of which they are now so proud.
I suppose, for instance, that Trafalgar Day (the day of his
death) is a public *fête* and that the towns in the provinces
throughout the country are proud to keep statues of him in
their market-places." " Not a bit of it," was the reply, "except
in Trafalgar Square I hardly know where to find a single
statue of him anywhere.   It is true that they have christened
a few, a very few 'pubs' (inns) after him, but even of these
there are far more called after Wellington. Wellington is the
man whose statues they like to put up." "But, great Heavens
above us," exclaimed the shade, at last losing every vestige of
patience, "what on earth did he do compared to the other
man of 171 hand-to-hand battles?" "Well, he won the battle of
Waterloo," replied the other.   "Won the battle of Waterloo!"
cried the shade in tones of intense disgust.   "What was his
share in it? He led the soldiers into an impossible place
where there was only one road in case of a retreat (which
was a great tactical error), and afterwards your guards and
infantry did the rest by holding their position all day and
suffering themselves to be killed rather than retire.   What
part did the General play compared to that of the Admiral
at the battle of Trafalgar?   The thing is absurd! You
Englishmen are, as we all know, a nation of merchants
and thoroughly agree with my own maxim during my life
that solid prosperity is much better than fame and glory,
but you owe the bulk of your nation's riches to your mercantile shipping trade and you owe the bulk of that to the

deeds of Nelson, which gave you the dominion of the seas. Bah! the whole thing is ridiculous; *c'est le comble de la bêtise.*"

Our modern maritime empire is largely the shadow cast by the life of one great man, Horatio Nelson. This man chiefly did the work by means of men of a class obscure and unheeded both then and now, viz. the smacksmen and trawlers of Norfolk and Suffolk. These men, accustomed from childhood to struggle with the tides, storms, and cold of the North Sea, and to endure hardships unknown to other classes, in silence and with but a trifling money reward, laboured, fought, and often died in making the Empire.

FINIS

For EU product safety concerns, contact us at Calle de José Abascal, 56–1°,
28003 Madrid, Spain or eugpsr@cambridge.org.

www.ingramcontent.com/pod-product-compliance
Ingram Content Group UK Ltd.
Pitfield, Milton Keynes, MK11 3LW, UK
UKHW012341130625
459647UK00009B/455